Yordan Yovkov

Yordan Yovkov

by

Edward Możejko

The University of Alberta

Slavica Publishers, Inc.
Columbus, Ohio

Slavica publishes a wide variety of books and journals dealing with the peoples, languages, literatures, history, folklore, and culture of the peoples of Eastern Europe and the USSR. For a complete catalog with prices and ordering information, please write to:

Slavica Publishers, Inc.
P.O. Box 14388
Columbus, Ohio 43214
USA

ISBN: 0-89357-117-2.

This book was published in 1984.

Text set by Kathleen McDermott at the East European Composition Center, supported by the Department of Slavic Languages and Literatures and the Center for Russian and East European Studies at UCLA.

Printed in the United States of America.

CONTENTS

Preface

In 1980 occurred the hundredth anniversary of the birth of Yordan Yovkov
— one of the greatest storytellers Bulgaria has ever produced. This provided a golden opportunity to stimulate interest in his writing both at home
and abroad. Indeed, the Bulgarian Union of Writers and the Bulgarian
Academy of Sciences organized scholarly sessions and official celebrations
to commemorate this great writer, artist and humanist; in November 1980
Bulgarian publications allotted much space to various aspects of Yovkov's
work. However, oddly enough no full-length book appeared which would
give a comprehensive discussion of all Yovkov's writing. Thus, since the
publication of Simeon Sultanov's book in 1968, no extensive study on Yovkov has come out. That is very little for a writer of such stature.

This book makes a modest attempt to fill that gap, to pay tribute to
Yovkov's literary genius, and to introduce him to the English-speaking
reader.

The suggestion that I write this monograph came from Charles Moser of
the George Washington University, and I would like to express here my
sincere gratitude for his patient encouragement. I must admit that I under-
took the task with some hesitation. My first publication on Yovkov
appeared 16 years ago, in Poland. Although occasionally I returned to
Yovkov, my scholarly interests gradually drifted away from both him and
Bulgarian literature in general, so that I was out of contact with him. What
would a renewed acquaintance do? Would it confirm my previous admiration, or bring disappointment? Would it be like meeting an old friend
whose wrinkles remind us of the relentless passage of time, or like running
into an old love for whom feeling cannot be revived? My second encounter
with Yovkov eliminated all these apprehensions. Not only did I find Yovkov even more exciting than ever, I found him also much "deeper" in the
philosophical sense of the word, and — paradoxically — much more
"modern"; he keeps pace with our time. My second "discovery" of Yovkov
confirmed again my longstanding belief that world literature cannot be
divided into the categories of so-called "great" literatures (e.g. English,
French, Russian) and "small" literatures; the demarcation line in world
literature should separate "great writers" and "secondary writers," because
"small" literatures are capable of producing writers just as fine as those to
be found in "great" literatures.

Since Yovkov is practically unknown in the West, in this monograph I
have dealt with almost every important theme of his prose and dramas:
war, love, the cult of patriarchal tradition, beauty, and so on. This study is

composed of five chapters. Chapter one is entirely devoted to Yovkov's biography. Information about his life is scattered through many publications, and has never been gathered into one systematic whole within a larger study. The subsequent chapters deal with the war prose (II), the prose of the 1920's (III), and plays (IV). The last chapter covers short stories and the novels of the 1930's. By and large the book should give an adequate picture of Yovkov as man and writer. Since only a few of his short stories have been translated into English, I provide extensive plot summaries of some of his works, thereafter adding interpretation and sometimes analysis of his artistic craft. All translations of quotations from Yovkov's works except one (done by Professor Moser) are mine. On the other hand, for the sake of consistency I have used (whenever possible) the English titles of Yovkov's works found in Professor Moser's *History of Bulgarian Literature 865–1944* (1972), and his article on Yovkov published in *The Slavic and East European Journal* in 1967. I owe much to those publications.

July 1981   Edmonton, Alberta, Canada

Acknowledgments

I would like to express my warmest gratitude to Dr. Francis Macri of Edmonton for his generous and understanding editing of my English text. He cannot be praised enough for his contribution to the final version of this book. My thanks go also to Sheila Steinhauer for her time-consuming and painstaking proofreading of the typed manuscript. And last but definitely not least I would like to express my special thanks to Mrs. Doreen Hawryshko for her devoted typing and her help with the final preparation of this book.

Chronology

1880   November 9: Yordan Yovkov born in the village of Zheravna, the fifth child of shepherd and landowner Stefan Yovkov and Pena Yovkova.

1880   Yovkov's father settles in the village of Chifutkyoy, in Dobrudzha. The family stays behind in Zheravna.

1887   Enters Zheravna's elementary school.

1893   Moves to Ruse to continue his elementary education; lives there with his brother, Nikolay.

1895   Back in Zheravna, Yovkov repeats the last year of junior high school (1895–96).

1896   Leaves Zheravna for good, enters high school in Kotel.

1897   Moves to Sofia to continue his high school education in the capital, living with his brother Nikolay.

1900   Graduates from the I Sofia Gymnasium, appointed as a teacher in Chiflik Musubey, near the village where his parents lived.

1902   Enters the military academy for reserve officers in Knyazhevo, near Sofia. Makes his literary debut in October.

1904   Enrolls in the Faculty of Law. His father dies, and Yovkov returns to Dobrudzha to become a teacher again in Chiflik Musubey.

1906   Appointed as a teacher at the elementary school in Sarudzha.

1907   Moves to Karalii, where in 1909 he becomes the principal of a newly founded junior high school. Remains there until the outbreak of the Balkan War in 1912.

1910   Yovkov's first story, "The Shepherd's Plaint," is published.

1912   Outbreak of the First Balkan War. Yovkov joins the army.

1913   Death of Yovkov's mother.

1914   In Sofia he meets for the first time poets and writers Nikolay Liliev, Dimitur Podvurzachov, Konstantin Konstantinov, and Georgi Raychev.

1915   Back in the army, but after six months on the Greek border he returns to Sofia to become a regular war correspondent for various periodicals.

1917   Yovkov's first volume of war prose published under the title *Short Stories*.

1918   His second volume of stories appears. The war ends, and Yovkov leaves the army with the rank of captain. He returns to Dobrudzha to marry Despina Koleva, a former teacher whom he had met earlier in Sofia.

1919   Birth of their only child, Elka.

1920   Diplomatic appointment as a press official with the Bulgarian legation in Bucharest.

1927   *Balkan Legends* published. The same year returns to Sofia.

1928   *Evenings at the Antimovo Inn.*

1929   His first drama, *Albena*, staged at the National Theater in Sofia.

1930   Begins writing the novel *Gorolomov's Adventures*. It remained unfinished, but appeared posthumously as a book in 1938.

1935   *A Woman's Heart* published.

1936   *If They Could Speak* published in Sofia.

1937   October 15: Yovkov dies of cancer in Plovdiv's Catholic Hospital.

CHAPTER 1

The Biography

In various literary anthologies and biographies, Yovkov is said to have been born on one of five different dates: November 8, 1884 (commonly acepted in the 1920's and 1930's); November 8, 1881; November 8, 1880; November 9, 1880; and December 9, 1880. It is unclear why this confusion arose.[1] There is a strong suspicion that Yovkov himself was responsible for it. This fact, though not important in itself, reflects to some extent on the whole life of this writer — an individual withdrawn in his own world of dreams, jealously guarding his privacy and only reluctantly communicating his thoughts to others. When attempts were made to clarify this matter,[2] Yovkov insisted that it should be left as it was. He admitted the existing error, but suggested that nothing be done to rectify it until his death.[3] He maintained that "historical" truth would be established if the memory of him and his literary work survived.

Indeed, Yovkov was right. The first critic to publish the correct date of his birth was Georgi Konstantinov,[4] and then in 1941, four years after the writer's death. His findings were confirmed by Dimo Minev in his excellent collection of documents, still the best source of information about Yovkov: *Yordan Yovkov: Dokumenti i svidetelstva za zhivota i tvorchestvoto mu*[5] (Yordan Yovkov. Documents and Testimonies About His Life and Writings), published in 1947. Minev was the first to bring to light the evidence of Yovkov's birth certificate, preserved by his younger brother, Kosta Yovkov.

According to this document, Yovkov was born on November 9, 1880, to the family of Stefan and Pena Yovkov. He was the second of six siblings (five sons and one daughter) that included Yosif, Nikolay, Suba, Boycho, Yordan and Kosta.

Zheravna, the place of Yovkov's birth, is a middle-sized village situated on the slopes of the Eastern Balkan range. According to Danail Konstantinov,[6] etymologically the name Zheravna is of Greek origin, stemming from the word Zerbon, which means "left-handed." During the time of the Byzantine yoke in the XI–XII centuries, it was the name of a creek that traversed the settlement.[7] This picturesque area has many small rivers, springs, ravines and creeks, and it is no wonder that Zheravna derived its name from one of them. Many topographical names in the Zheravna area recur later in Yovkov's finest collection of stories, *Staroplaninski legendi* (Balkan Legends).[8] This area has preserved much of its primordial ruggedness, charm and magnificence. Its romantic and adventurous past inspired the writer's imagination, thus contributing to the thematic richness of Bulgarian literature. When I visited Zheravna in 1960, on the occasion of the 80th anniversary of Yovkov's birth, I was overpowered by its atmosphere of romantic serenity. It emanated not only from the small, unpaved streets of the village and its poor houses, but also from the eyes of Zheravna's inhabitants.

Traditionally, the population of Zheravna followed trades that tied them closely to nature. Farming, cattle-breeding and shepherding were the primary occupations. As a young boy Yovkov's father, Stefan, was sent to learn the craft of wool-weaving, but instead he began to earn his living as a shepherd. According to his son Kosta,[9] he broke with custom and changed from wearing traditional "Turkish" clothes, consisting of *poturi*[10] and *saltamarka,*[11] to modern "French" (as they were called in Bulgaria at the time) trousers, jacket, shirt and tie. He was known around Zheravna as an energetic and diligent man. As a consequence, Stefan Yovkov managed to acquire quite a substantial fortune. In the late 1870's he moved to the Romanian part of Northern Dobrudzha, where nature had created favorable conditions for both farming and cattle-breeding. In 1880, he settled in the village of Chifutkyoy, just south of the border, on the Bulgarian side of divided Dobrudzha.[12] There he bought land for farming and continued shepherding until his death in 1904. However, for quite a period of time Stefan Yovkov maintained two homes: one in Zheravna (where he also owned an old inn), and one in Chifutkyoy. From Chifutkyoy he used to bring back to Zheravna wool which his wife wove into fabric for both domestic and commercial use. The rest of the family joined him permanently in Chifutkyoy as late as 1897.

Throughout all these years, Pena Yovkova was a stable and never-failing support to her husband, and also for the entire family. Staying at home with the children in Zheravna, she became the reliable element of the household, lending it a sense of stability and order. Although illiterate herself, she was a lively and intelligent person whose extensive knowledge of folklore was generally admired. She knew by heart hundreds of folk songs which she sometimes performed at social gatherings, called *sedênki*. It is often said that Yovkov inherited from his father an inner discipline, a certain aloofness, and a fondness for neatness. However, there is every reason to believe that the writer's ties with his mother were much stronger, and especially important for the shaping of his creative individuality. For example, from her he developed a love of folklore which played such an important role in his writing.

Little is known about Yovkov's relations with his siblings, but everything points to a rather loose relationship between them. Some of them died relatively young. The only sister, Suba, passed away in her thirties, and one brother, Nikolay, at the age of 39. With him Yovkov seems to have established a relatively close relationship. He lived with him twice: once in Ruse, a city on the banks of the Danube River on the Romanian border (where Yordan continued his junior high school [*progimnaziya*] education in 1893–94); and again in Sofia, where he graduated from high school in 1900. Yovkov obtained his last two years of secondary education in the capital, and we can understand why the writer developed a strong attachment to this older brother, nine years his senior. Nikolay was by far the best educated among Yovkov's siblings. Although a clerk by profession (he worked in Ruse as a customs official and in Sofia as a bank clerk), Nikolay was interested in social questions as well as art and literature. He was closely associated with the left-wing social-democratic movement, the so-called "narrow socialists" who laid the foundations for the future Bulgarian Communist Party. He was a personal friend of the founders and leaders of the movement, Dimitur Blagoev and Georgi Kirkov.

Yovkov never shared his brother's leftist convictions, preferring to remain aloof from social and political activity. His schoolmates, friends and family unanimously depict him as a joyful but at the same time contemplative type. In all probability, there existed between the two brothers a general intellectual affinity deriving from their common interest in the humanities. On this ground, no doubt, they found common interests, regardless of how they interpreted them. Thus Nikolay was not only capable of understanding his younger brother's artistic and literary ambitions, but was also willing to help him with his education.

Whatever may be said about the writer's relationship with his closest relatives, one thing seems certain: the fact that he lived with his family in two different regions of Bulgaria left an indelible imprint on his literary imagination and decisively affected his artistic evolution. Zheravna's old romantic legends and the wisdom of Dobrudzha's peasants were two inexhaustible sources for Yovkov's inspiration. The seemingly trivial life of people in two remote regions of Bulgaria acquired meaning under the writer's pen and was transformed into a literature of time and place that may be compared to the work of William Faulkner.

Yovkov left Zheravna in 1896, after finishing elementary school and the first two years of junior high school from 1890 to 1893. Since no third year (grade seven, if we count consecutive years of schooling) was offered[13] in Zheravna, Yovkov moved to Ruse. The new environment and higher scholastic standards proved difficult for him. Yovkov's accomplishments were poor, not to say disastrous: he barely passed his examinations. Disenchanted by this experience, he almost dropped out of school. The next school year, 1894–95, Yovkov spent with his parents in Chifutkyoy. In the meantime, the third year was introduced in Zheravna and the boy's parents decided he should repeat it there if he wanted to proceed with his education at the *gymnasium*. Yovkov returned to Zheravna and spent 1895–96 in his native village.[14] In 1896 Yovkov entered high school in Kotel, and thereafter moved to Sofia to finish the last three years in the capital.

Yovkov's biographers tell us that in the last four years of high school he developed a very keen interest in literature. Apart from Bulgarian writers — such as Ivan Vazov, Khristo Botev and Aleko Konstantinov — the young Yovkov was well acquainted with Victor Hugo, Ivan Turgenev, Leo Tolstoy and Nikolay Gogol. While in Sofia, he followed closely the contemporary evolution of literature, witnessing the oncoming triumph of Modernism in both Russia and Bulgaria.

III   THE MAN, TEACHER AND WRITER

Literature, however, did not attract Yovkov as a subject of study. Shortly after graduating in Sofia, Yovkov entered the military academy for reserve officers in Knyazhevo near the capital, because he wanted to serve in the military rather than wait to be drafted. In all probability, he also wanted to gain some time before deciding on his future, as he was not certain what profession he would enter. For a short while he seriously considered the study of painting[15] at the school of fine arts in Sofia, but dropped the idea in favor of a more practical profession — law. Yovkov entered the Faculty of Law at the University of Sofia in early 1904. However, his work in law was of short duration. Yovkov attended lectures for one semester only and did not take any examinations. In the summer of 1904, he left the capital to become a teacher in Dobrudzha. Probably he did this for a variety of reasons. There is no doubt that after his father's death in 1904, Yovkov felt he should live closer to his mother. There was, however, another and more important reason for his move to Dobrudzha: his increasing awareness that his true vocation was literature. Law would distract him from writing, because both study and legal practice would have been time-consuming. Moreover, teaching would bring him closer to people, and give him a better chance to observe and participate in the everyday life of the peasants — a class of people whom Yovkov admired for their ability to preserve rustic customs and patriarchal moral values. Indeed, living among the peasantry gave Yovkov a deeper insight into their habits, their psychology, their joys and sorrows; he became acquainted with their philosophy of life and made it his own. He accepted their understanding of such universal values as good and evil, which later played an important role in his prose.

Yovkov was appointed as elementary school teacher for the first time in 1900, immediately upon finishing high school, and entered the profession without a teaching certificate qualifying him for the job. He taught for one year in Chiflik Musubey (now Dolen Izvor), not far from the village where his parents lived. He did not, however, resume his duties in 1901–1903, as he wished to enter military service in Knyazhevo. When he returned to Dobrudzha in 1904, he resumed teaching in Chiflik Musubey, remaining there until 1906. In the fall of 1906 Yovkov started in Sarudzha (now Rositsa), and in 1907 he moved to Karalii (now Krasen), where he remained until joining the army in the fall of 1912. Initially he worked there as a teacher, but in 1909, when the school was turned into a junior high school, Yovkov became its first principal.

Thanks to Minev's documentary book, we now know a great deal about Yovkov's personality and life in Dobrudzha. Out of Minev's meticulous collection of documents, archival records and recollections from the writer's relatives, friends, colleagues, and pupils emerges an interesting but controversial character: pensive on the one hand but cheerful, prone to amusement on the other; open and honest with his friends and colleagues but at the same time very secretive, so that he created a kind of mystery around himself; courting female teachers but never ready to accept rejection; almost morbidly jealous of other men. This enumeration of contradictory characteristics could be extended. What is more important, however, is the fact that Yovkov was highly respected as a knowledgeable man and a good teacher — rigorous but fair.

According to many witnesses interviewed by Minev, Yovkov led a very ordinary life while a teacher in Dobrudzha. He participated in teachers' meetings and took part in the activity of their association, but he never evinced any particular enthusiasm for his profession or things associated with it. In fact, one teacher with whom Yovkov was quite friendly during his years in Dobrudzha maintained that the young writer disliked his profession and adopted a slightly derisive attitude towards his colleagues. Two reasons are advanced for Yovkov's failure to leave Dobrudzha. First, he

found living in the country interesting and liked the peasants' simple way
of life. And furthermore he lacked the necessary resolve to move elsewhere
until the outbreak of war in 1912 compelled him to change his hitherto
convenient way of life.[16]

Yovkov's involvement with the teachers' union was of a rather haphaz-
ard nature, but it occasionally brought him into conflict with his colleagues. He was a member of the Radical Party[17] and his political views
sometimes tinged his stand on both professional and union issues. Y. Bel-
chev, another teacher from Sofia and a member of the Social-Democratic
Party (the so-called "broad socialists") recalls that his differences with
Yovkov during a congress of teachers in Dobrich were mainly of a political
nature.

Yovkov's involvement in social matters never constituted an essential
part of his life, wherever he was in the villages of Dobrudzha. Instead he
displayed a predilection which proved to be much more important for the
formation of his individuality as a creative writer: his passion for learning
about people regardless of their nationality (Bulgarians, Turks, Romanians,
and gypsies all lived in Dobrudzha). He helped farmers write official letters
to the authorities; he read historical books to elderly people and listened
to their stories; he liked to sit for hours in old inns observing the peasants'
behavior, sometimes joining in their celebrations. He was genuinely interested in books, and subscribed to various literary publications and journals. He read whatever was available in local libraries and from friends:
Henrik Ibsen, Gerhardt Hauptmann, Maxim Gorky, Stanislaw Przybys-
zewski, Leo Tolstoy, Ivan Turgenev, Fedor Dostoevsky, Nikolay Gogol,
Mikhail Lermontov, Nikolay Nekrasov, and — among Bulgarian authors
— Elin Pelin, Pencho Slaveykov, and Ivan Vazov.

As an individual Yovkov displayed quite a few eccentricities. He was an
incorrigible chain-smoker who spent hours in isolation smoking cigarettes
and reading books. He liked to hunt, but as a rule used up his supply of
cartridges long before sighting any real target by shooting into the air: he
found that much more relaxing than killing wild animals, and often
returned home as soon as his cartridge-belt was empty. He was also known
for another strange habit: during long hours of loneliness and boredom in
the small villages of Dobrudzha, where there was little to do, Yovkov
would lie on his bed and fire at the ceiling. Traces of this rather unusual
exercise were still visible in the 1960's in certain rooms where he lived as a
teacher.

Everyone interviewed by Minev agreed that Yovkov loved to dress very
neatly, with good taste and according to the latest fashion. He spared no

expense on clothes, and liked to pique a woman's fancy. In general, he had a fine esthetic sense. While in Dobrudzha, Yovkov was interested in a number of women, but none of his relationships ended in marriage. One reason may have been that he was very possessive, and this often turned women away from him. One of his friends, Yordanka Simeonova, although in love with the writer, could not marry him because her father thought him too poor.[18]

Whatever we may say about Yovkov's personal life, at least one thing seems certain: he was passionately committed to literature. His literary debut came shortly after his graduation from high school, when his first poem, "Under A Child's Cross" appeared in the journal *Suznanie* (Consciousness) in October 1902. His colleagues knew of his literary interests, and occasionally read his poems and short stories published in such periodicals as *Khudozhnik* (Artist), *Prosveta* (Education), *Selska probuda* (Rural Awakening), *Novo obshtestvo* (New Society), *Nash zhivot* (Our Life), and *Nablyudatel* (Observer). Sometimes he spoke quite openly about his obsession with literature. A friend recalled that in a conversation with Yovkov the latter told her, "Don't take me for what I am now. I shall become famous because I feel my strength."[20]

Little is known about Yovkov's intellectual growth at the beginning of the century. His literary biographers tend to omit this period of his life in order to pass directly to an analysis of his war prose and his accomplishments of the 1920's and 1930's. Indeed, Yovkov himself spoke reluctantly about this period of his creative activity, and rightly so: neither his poetry nor his prose in that early period was especially distinguished. Later on, when an established author, Yovkov categorically forbade publishers to include his early literary output in the collections of his works that appeared in the 1920's and 1930's. He made but one exception: he included "Ovcharova zhalba" (The Shepherd's Plaint, 1910), after considerable stylistic modification, in his collection *Balkan Legends* (1927). Despite Yovkov's objections, the early period of his literary career deserves mention because it reveals Yovkov's connections with literary tendencies of the time. It is clear that during those years, Yovkov developed a very individualistic perception of reality which reflected the influence of what has been defined in the history of literature as Modernism.[21] Many writers — including those who espoused Realism in art, such as Elin Pelin in Bulgaria — found themselves under the sway of Modernism at that time. In the twenty-two poems Yovkov published between 1902 and 1910, the attitude of the poetic persona is that of a disenchanted intellectual who gloomily observes the world he lives in. His poetry did not shine with originality: he borrowed many motifs from the Bulgarian Symbolist poet Peyo Yavorov.[22] His style is rhetorical and turgid. His symbols are offensively naive. In the poem "Prolet" (Spring), the title is supposed to point to a mysterious, enchanting beauty; "man" is compared to Sisyphus, who knocks in vain at the gates of happiness; "autumn" embodies grief and despair. The banality of such symbols derives from a lack of authentic poetic experience on the part of the poetic persona. For Yavorov the struggle of good and evil, of happiness and sorrow constitutes the very essence of his poetry because it expresses his own personal obsession, but in Yovkov's poetry the same motifs are artificial, devoid of any authenticity. The almost programmatic pessimism of these poems amounts to an affectation that appears to be a remote echo of the work of other, more talented Symbolists, such as Nikolay Liliev or Teodor Trayanov, and, of course, Yavorov.

Fortunately, by 1910, Yovkov realized that poetry was not his vocation, and Bulgarian literature gained a great storyteller as it lost a mediocre poet. However, it should be added that the somber perception of the world in Yovkov's poetry carried over into his prose. Of thirteen short stories published between 1910 and 1913 (that is, from Yovkov's prose debut to the time when his first war stories were published), only two were written in a more optimistic tone. In almost all of them Yovkov exhibits a predilection for psychological character analysis. As a rule, his characters exhibit pathological features, and deviate in their behavior from what is generally considered to be normal. In "Sinite minzukhari" (The Blue Crocus), the author describes the hopeless love of a deaf-mute for a girl, Rusana. If the choice of theme is unusual, the situations created in the story are even more out of the ordinary: they are designed to sketch a psychological portrait of the deaf-mute. The short story "Tuga" (Sorrow), which contains some autobiographical details, is a prime example of Yovkov's pessimism and liking for psychological analysis. A lonely teacher, Andrey, moves from a village to a city; unable to adjust to his new surroundings, he feels alienated and lost. His sense of loneliness is deepened by the sudden death of his sister (both events happened in Yovkov's life: he moved to the city and his sister, Suba, died). All the typical elements of Symbolist poetics are assembled in this story: moodiness, strangeness, the allegorical meaning of symbols. A gloomy atmosphere of impending doom permeates it; crows and black clouds herald ill fortune. The author uses interior monologue in order to dig deeper into his hero's subconscious and to reveal his spiritual turmoil.

The hero of these stories is usually a disappointed teacher or intellectual who rebels against the world as an advocate of extreme individualism. We find such characters in "Edin esenen den" (On An Autumn Day), "Bez myasto" (Without a Place), "Sled prolet" (After Spring). He is entirely absorbed by his own internal life, unhappy, isolated from or rejected by his social milieu. Generally speaking, a tendency to create moody situations is one of the main characteristics of Yovkov's early prose. He creates settings which suggest a correlation between psychological frame of mind and natural phenomena. The external world — night, storm, cloudy sky, crows and so on — foretells the course of action. The Symbolists inherited this artistic device from Romanticism, and Yovkov made extensive use of it in his early literary activity. Later on, it shapes the narration of his war stories, but on a considerably modified and more limited basis.

Yovkov's early writing is of more interest biographically than as a part of his artistic achievement, which is why he never agreed to its inclusion in any collections of his work. After this preparatory exercise in creative writing, his real literary apprenticeship begins with the publication of the first war sketches in 1913.

When the First Balkan War broke out in the fall of 1912, Yovkov immediately joined the army. At first he served as aide-de-camp to the commander of the 41st infantry regiment but shortly thereafter was transferred at his own request to the staff of the commanding officer of the 5th company in the same regiment. Yovkov preferred it that way. Being an aide-de-camp meant he took no part in combat: he disliked the thought. According to his younger brother Kosta,[23] who served during this campaign in the same regiment, Yovkov experienced his baptism of fire on October 9, 1912, at the village of Kaypa, near Odrin (now Edirne, a border town in the western part of Turkey). With drawn sword he led his three hundred men against Turkish positions in a successful assault. The writer's war adventures continued throughout the Second Balkan War, during which time he was wounded in the legs and discharged. Yet Yovkov could not return to his beloved Dobrudzha: as a consequence of the war, Southern Dobrudzha, including the village of Chifutkyoy where his mother lived (she died the very day the Romanian occupation began — July 13, 1913) and other villages in which he had taught prior to enlisting became part of Romania. Yovkov "became an exile in his own country." He went to Sofia, where he met many of his fellow countrymen from Dobrudzha; but his career as a writer gained far more from encounters with young and rising celebrities of modern Bulgarian literature, including Nikolay Liliev, Dimitur Podvurzachov, Georgi Raychev, and Konstantin Konstantinov. Yovkov contracted close and lifelong friendships with some of them, especially Liliev and Podvurzachov. In 1914 they published one of the most important almanacs of Bulgarian Symbolism — *Zveno* (Link). In the same year he published his first important short stories about the war.

The interim period of peace between the end of the Balkan Wars (July 1913) and the beginning of World War I was short. In 1915 Bulgaria joined the Central Powers and declared war against Serbia and Greece. Yovkov was drafted again as a reserve officer with the rank of lieutenant, after being promoted to this rank during the Balkan Wars, and decorated with the Order for Bravery. He spent six months on the Greek-Bulgarian border, but this time participated in no battles. In 1915 he was called back to Sofia to work as a war correspondent for various journals and periodicals,[24] and remained there until the end of the war.

While Yovkov greeted the Balkan Wars with considerable enthusiasm — as did the average Bulgarian — his attitude toward the World War was more negative. He feared that it might bring the country to another and even worse disaster. The outcome of the war confirmed his misgivings. The territories Bulgaria had regained during the military operations of 1915–18 had to be ceded once more; the country was compelled to accept foreign occupation and pay considerable war reparations.

The final loss of Southern Dobrudzha as a result of the World War was a personal tragedy for the writer. Yovkov entered a period of deep spiritual crisis which to a great extent determined the future course of his writing. Those who knew him before the wars, and then again in 1918–19, speak of him as two different individuals. The change was so obvious that the critic Simeon Sultanov writes[25] about "two Yovkovs": the "young" one and the "grown-up." By nature, Yovkov was rather introverted, but those who knew him in Dobrudzha were often amazed by his openness, his sense of humor, and his ability to cultivate relations with others, to cherish friend-ship, to show joy and displeasure. All these features of his individuality vanished, as it were, after the war. He withdrew into the world of his own thoughts and dreams, became somber and very reluctant to meet people. The rout of 1918 left the writer bitter and disappointed to the point of misanthropy. As the former mayor of Dobrich (Tolbukhin), who met Yov-kov in 1918–1919 wrote:

> He was terribly shattered by the national catastrophe. He was as shattered as a soldier from the front would be who had seen the imprudence of rulers and the helplessness of diplomats. His soul was depressed and he was seized with total despair. He withdrew into himself, seldom went out into the streets and social haunts, and commented on events among his closest friends only.... For him this period must have been decisive. Withdrawn into himself, ... he wrote at that time his most beautiful works.[26]

As soon as Yovkov moved to Sofia, another complex assaulted him, one which obsessed him to the end of his life, but was particularly painful in the first years after the war. This was the complex of a newcomer to the city. Here is what Yovkov himself had to say on the matter:

> I am considered to be taciturn. This is completely untrue. I gave the appearance of being such when I found myself in an environment that was entirely alien to me. I came from the provinces and always felt as if I were a guest here and would return where I had come from.[27]

On the one hand he felt uprooted from his own natural milieu; on the other, he needed the cultural atmosphere of the city for his own creative development. He felt ill at ease among city people, and the ambiguity of his feelings did not contribute to his psychological stability.

However, the worst of experiences came the very day Yovkov left the army: he was jobless, unwanted and rejected, a virtual burden on society, like many other nameless heroes who experienced total humiliation. His case was even worse because he had never acquired a profession, and a self-made teacher had little chance of obtaining a position after the war, when jobs were scarce and new regulations called for certificates in education, which Yovkov did not have. Still, friends managed to find him a teaching position in one of Varna's upper schools. It was a kind of sinecure, but Yovkov soon realized he did not like the teaching profession at all and resigned from the job.

As if this were not enough, Yovkov at that time was newly married. He had been married in the autumn of 1918 in Dobrich (this was his last visit to Dobrudzha) to Despina Koleva, fifteen years his junior, whom he had met in Sofia. In 1919 their daughter Elka was born, and Yovkov desperately needed a stable income to support his family. He applied for several jobs in Sofia, without success, until, thanks to the intercession of friends again, he was offered the insignificant post of press official in the foreign service. He accepted it as a necessary evil, because he could see no other way to improve his material situation. The Ministry of Foreign Affairs offered him a choice of three diplomatic posts: Switzerland, the United States, and Romania. He chose the latter, as it was closest to his homeland.

One would expect that after so many unpleasant experiences the writer might have found some peace of mind and relief from financial difficulties. Quite to the contrary: on September 30, 1921, after a change in the government, Yovkov was fired, a victim of partisan politics and intrigue. Fortunately, however, this decision was reversed and Yovkov continued to work at the Bulgarian Legation in Bucharest until 1927. These were not, however, happy years in the writer's life. He was overloaded with stupefying administrative duties. Nobody thought of giving him more time for his creative writing, and his salary was so low that it hardly allowed the family to make ends meet. The situation improved somewhat when Despina Yovkova became a teacher at the school for Bulgarian children in Bucharest, but their living conditions still left much to be desired. His financial difficulties in the Romanian capital cropped up constantly in Yovkov's conversations with friends. To one of them he openly confessed that he "lived in horrible conditions."[28] He also alluded to it in some official letters he wrote to his superiors.[29] Intrigue and unpleasantness plagued Yovkov as a diplomat to the very end of his sojourn in Bucharest. In 1922 he was promoted to the rank of secretary at the Bulgarian Consulate in Odessa "while retaining his duties at the Legation in Bucharest." However, in 1925 Yovkov suffered one of the worst blows imaginable for a devoted official : he was degraded to the position of ordinary translator (*dragoman*) on a reduced salary. It is no wonder then, that during this period Yovkov developed a mysterious stomach illness that later became a fatal ailment. The writer had complained often in the past of stomach pains; now they became almost permanent. His exhaustion reached a point at which he felt compelled to leave Bucharest and return to Bulgaria. He submitted his resignation on October 21, 1927.

It should be remembered here that from the standpoint of his creative evolution the "Romanian period" in Yovkov's life was very fruitful. Yovkov, indeed, showed remarkable fortitude. In spite of all his material difficulties, in Bucharest he wrote some of his finest collections of short stories: *Balkan Legends, Posledna radost* (Last Joy), *Vecheri v antimovskiya khan* (Evenings at the Antimovo Inn).

The last decade in Sofia (1927–1937) was probably the happiest period in Yovkov's life. He achieved relative financial security and recognition as a writer. His resignation from his post in Bucharest in fact meant a transfer, for he remained employed in the press section in the Ministry of Foreign Affairs to the very end of his life. In this capacity he served on the editorial boards of *La Bulgarie* and *Novi dni* (New Days), governmental publications which promoted Bulgarian cultural achievements both abroad and inside the country. This last period in Yovkov's life is also his most prolific in terms of literary output. He wrote four plays, two novels, two collections of short stories, and revised his novelette *Zhetvaryut* (The Harvester).

That made his sudden and untimely death all the more tragic. Doctors were unable to discover the real nature of his chronic stomach disorder, and in 1937 things turned worse. In October of that year Yovkov decided to go to the resort of Khisarya, where mineral waters might improve his deteriorating health. The opposite happened: his condition rapidly worsened, and he died on October 15, 1937. Among those at his bedside were his wife, the writer and critic Vicho Ivanov, and the now well-known historian of literature Petur Dinekov,[30] then an aspiring literary critic. An autopsy performed in Plovdiv's Catholic Hospital showed Yovkov had a tumor. Apparently he died of cancer. The day of his burial in Sofia was declared a day of national mourning.

CHAPTER 2

The War Prose

I YOVKOV AND THE WAR

Yovkov's sojourn in Dobrudzha from 1904 to the outbreak of the first Balkan War in 1912 had a decisive impact on the further evolution of his writing. During this time Yovkov recognized in the depth and wealth of rural life a possible source of literary inspiration. At the end of this period he consciously looked for material that would lend itself to transformation into fiction and reflect his experience and knowledge of the peasants of Dobrudzha. He moved towards a more realistic type of writing, the first fruit of which was the story "A Shepherd's Plaint," which marked the end of his interest in poetry. As we have seen in the previous chapter, Yovkov's early prose still remained under the strong influence of the Symbolist literary tradition. However, the very fact that Yovkov abandoned poetry for prose is significant in its own right. As a literary movement, Symbolism favored poetry over prose, but Yovkov realized that modern poetry could not serve as a proper vehicle for the expression of his basically realistic experiences and observations. Faced with a dilemma — either to comply with the demands of Symbolist literary poetics or to deviate and try to find his own voice — Yovkov opted for the latter. What he needed now was an inspiration that would shatter his Symbolist dreams, that would arouse him from the Symbolist lethargy, and let his talent shine with its own brilliance. The war gave him this impulse. In fact, some critics say war made Yovkov a writer.

In 1912 three Balkan countries — Bulgaria, Greece and Serbia — forged an alliance against Turkey, which still occupied a considerable part of the peninsula. The official slogan justifying this move proclaimed the idea of liberating the last parcel of European territory from the "Turkish yoke." Each country in the alliance expected territorial gain, and so the war was popular. Thus, Bulgaria claimed the right to liberate its brothers living in Macedonia, which Bulgarians considered part and parcel of their homeland. This goal evoked patriotic enthusiasm[1] of unprecedented dimensions, and Yovkov, like many of his peers, joined the army. At the time he did not suspect that the war, except for brief intervals, would last almost six years, and he was happy to participate in what he thought would be a historic conflict. Throughout the whole war Yovkov was particularly impressed by the bravery of the soldiers, most of them simple Bulgarian peasants. Their behavior stemmed from those moral values which Yovkov had come to hold in high esteem while living in Dobrudzha.

The First Balkan War was short. Under constant pressure from the allied forces, the Turkish army suffered a humiliating defeat, and peace was concluded in London on May 17, 1913. The main beneficiary of the treaty was Bulgaria, which gained control over the greater part of Macedonia, and thus came closer to realizing its historical objective of unifying all of Macedonia with the rest of the country.

The peace, however, did not last long. None of the parties to the London treaty was satisfied with what it had obtained. Greece and Serbia were convinced that Bulgaria had gained too much, while Bulgaria was unhappy at not having brought the whole of Macedonia under its control. The Bulgarian tsar, Ferdinand I, dreamed of conquering Istanbul and becoming the head of a new Bulgarian empire. In general, Bulgarian diplomacy of the time was quite clumsy and shortsighted, failing to foresee the possibility of a military confrontation with its former allies. True, both Greece and Serbia behaved provocatively by persecuting the population of occupied territories for its ties with Bulgaria. In this case the Bulgarian response should have been moderate, but instead Bulgaria took an aggressive position and triggered military operations. On June 16, 1913, roughly a month after the London treaty was concluded, Ferdinand ordered his troops to attack the positions of both Greek and Serbian forces, and the tragedy known as the Second Balkan War began. Greece, Serbia and Montenegro were joined by Turkey and Romania: Turkey wanted to regain at least a part of its lost territory, and Romania laid claim to Southern Dobrudzha. In the end, Bulgaria not only lost what it had gained in the First Balkan War, but also gave up part of its northern territory: that is, Southern Dobrudzha, Yovkov's country.

The war was a dramatic event in its own right, and called for artistic treatment. Consequently, it would be logical to ask how Yovkov saw the war and how he described it. Critics of all types agree that Yovkov is a great painter of battle scenes, and that few can match him in describing the vividness of war. However, the consensus ends at this point. As an author of war sketches and stories Yovkov contributed to what is generally termed war prose. The term itself is of relatively new coinage, although its tradition in modern times goes as far back as Leo Tolstoy. It grew out of the bloody, tragic experience of the two World Wars of this century. As a war-prose writer Yovkov has been compared to such authors as Erich

Maria Remarque, Vsevolod Garshin, and Henri Barbusse. Yovkov himself liked to emphasize his affinity with Tolstoy.[2] A comparison with each of the above-mentioned writers yields something different; and — though it may seem paradoxical — has helped to avoid an answer to the crucial question: was Yovkov for or against the war?

Bulgarian critics — in particular contemporary Marxist critics — are somewhat ambiguous in responding to this question. To say openly that the writer favored war would be disastrous, for then his writing — if not the whole of it, then at least the part devoted to the war — might be excluded from the mainstream of the national literature. Needless to say, that would be an irreparable cultural loss. There was no such ambiguity, however, in post-1945 Bulgarian Marxist literary criticism, which accused Yovkov of being a "reactionary" writer.[3] Equally extreme and unacceptable is the view expressed recently by Simeon Sultanov, who stresses Yovkov's alleged opposition to the war.[4] To be sure, one can find a few stories that would support such a claim: the truth is, however, that the author of *Zhetvaryat* (The Harvester, 1920) *accepted* the war when it broke out, and in some cases even became an apologist for it. He had a variety of reasons for doing so, none of which diminishes his greatness as a writer. First of all, Yovkov shared the sentiments of all Bulgarians in 1912 — he expected Macedonia to be liberated from Turkish domination. Second, he was, no doubt, fascinated by the dynamism and vivid character of battle: he looked at it with the eye of an artist. As a great writer he understood perfectly well that he could draw themes and motifs from something which, seen objectively, might be considered an evil.

To create beauty in literature does not necessarily mean to restrict oneself to morally acceptable examples of human behavior. Yovkov, the great moralist, distinguished clearly between such concepts as good and evil in life on the one hand, and the idea of artistic beauty on the other. He understood that the first two are in the domain of ethics, while the idea of beauty belongs to the sphere of esthetics. He confirmed his attitude later in one of his most interesting stories, "Albena."

There is yet another reason for Yovkov's presenting the war in a favorable light. We know that the Second Balkan War proved disastrous for Bulgaria. Territorially reduced, deprived of its gains made in 1912, Bulgaria emerged from the Second Balkan War politically humiliated, and almost immediately began to seek an opportunity for revenge. However, it was necessary to prepare the nation both morally and politically for yet another battle. To achieve this, the press began a campaign to spread a cult of heroism and soldierly sacrifice tinged with chauvinistic euphoria. The importance of isolated victories was exaggerated, and the causes for the defeat were analyzed. Wounded national pride found an outlet in extreme nationalism. Even such writers as Ivan Vazov and Kiril Khristov were caught up by this mood. In 1914 the journalist and writer Grigor Vasilev founded the journal *Narod i armiya* (Nation and Army) to promote patriotic feeling and to counteract the demoralization of some sections of Bulgarian public opinion. The journal's program, as formulated in an editorial in its first issue, was quite truculent. In fact, it amounted to open warmongering:

> The war against Turkey, and later against Serbia, Greece and Montenegro, will long remain the greatest national exploit. Its historical essence could be compared to that of the great French revolution. The consequences of the Balkan wars will not fade away with the signing of peace treaties. The whole future of the Balkan Peninsula will to a great extent depend on the result of the war. Peace now reigns again, but the struggle of the Balkan nations continues. It will not cease as long as human and national rights do not replace the slavery which still exists in Macedonia — and is even more terrible now. In these circumstances, the Bulgarian nation must be prepared for war if it does not wish to vanish. In the face of Europe it must be strong in its civilizing mission in the Balkans.[5]

Vasilev approached Yovkov and asked him to contribute to the journal. The writer readily accepted this opportunity to console his countrymen by describing the heroism of Bulgarian soldiers and their remarkable sense of duty. All his early stories — including "Utro na pametniya den" (Morning of a Memorable Day), "Otvud" (On the Other Side), "Purvata pobeda" (The First Victory), "Kaypa" (Kaypa), "Noshtite pred Odrin" (The Nights Before Odrin — later known as simply "Before Odrin") — were published in the pages of *Narod i armiya*. Later, Yovkov also published his war prose in *Voenni izvestiya* (Military News), *Otechestvo* (Fatherland), *Suvremenna misul* (Contemporary Thought), and *Demokraticheski pregled* (Democratic Review).

II   THE WAR IN THE STORIES

Yovkov's obvious commitment to the nationalist cause is confirmed by his writings: between the years 1914 and 1918 one can hardly find a story that promoted the idea of peace or protested the war. His three or four stories critical of the war — "Posledna radost" (Last Joy), "Belite rozi" (White Roses) and "Khermina" (Khermina) — were written after the war, in an entirely new historical situation, and quantitatively they constitute a very small part of Yovkov's war prose. On the basis of these few works one can hardly term Yovkov a writer who did nothing but protest the war, as Sultanov seems to imply, when there exist two volumes of his prose which present war in a favorable light. Consequently, Marxist criticism has adopted another approach to get around this difficulty. Efrem Karanfilov, in discussing Yovkov's war heroes,[6] applies in his analysis the well-known Marxist thesis (formulated by Engels) that permits a possible contradiction between a writer's world outlook and his creative method. Engels believed, for example, that despite Balzac's royalist sympathies and predilection for the *ancien régime*, he realistically described the rise of the new bourgeois social structure and the decline of the feudal system.[7] Lenin extended this thesis to Leo Tolstoy by pointing out the obvious contradiction between what he considered Tolstoy's reactionary religious world outlook and his progressive, realistic depiction of Russian society. Karanfilov utilizes the same device when he claims that Yovkov "often idealizes the war and its officers, and assails the enemy with rude words," while at the same time realistically describing Bulgarian soldiers, mostly peasants, whose behavior contrasts vividly with the "scurrying petty vanity and greedy preoccupation with getting rich and lucrative jobs" of the bourgeoisie. Unfortunately, Karanfilov does not support his assertion with any examples, and he is even less credible when he argues that Yovkov applies double ideological or moral criteria when describing soldiers and in presenting the other components of reality. Is there in fact a contradiction between the soldiers' perception of the war and that of Yovkov's narrator, in this case a quite faithful *alter ego*? To answer this question let us briefly examine the novelette *Zemlyatsi* (Fellow-Countrymen), one of the finest examples of Yovkov's war prose.

This is a story about four Dobrudzhan peasants drafted into the army to fight against the Turks during the Second Balkan War. There is little action, as the author concentrates primarily on describing their characters and the conditions under which the war is conducted. All four are highly individualized personalities. The peasant Stoil is deeply attached to the soil and the rural way of life; he is serious, almost philosophical, in his attitude towards life in general. Nikola is his opposite, a jester who lives for the moment, full of energy and comical inventiveness, playing the worldling, joking at the expense of others. The immediate butt of his humor is Dimitur, who shows an incredible indulgence for his ungrateful friend and puts up with his behavior without complaint. The humble Dimitur is not only "a good friend" to all soldiers, he also is noted for his bravery: he does not hesitate to volunteer for the most dangerous actions, and rumor has it that he is even so bold as to go out at night to rob dead enemy soldiers of their belongings, mainly tobacco. The least "distinctive," Iliya, is also the young-est. Formerly the company drummer, he lost his drum in one of the battles and is now an ordinary soldier. Like Dimitur with Stoil, so Iliya comple-ments Nikola's character. A cheerful individual who likes joking, though lacking Nikola's inventive spirit, he is content to be a graceful listener.

Together, Stoil, Nikola, Dimitur and Iliya embody the most valuable characteristics of Bulgarian soldiers: bravery, honesty, camaraderie, endur-ance. All four friends live in a dugout, for their military unit is conducting positional warfare. Step by step the author describes their chores, conversa-tions, and worries. Their daily routine consists primarily of visits with other soldiers, and petty quarrels; occasionally they exchange fire with the enemy. Once a week, on Sundays, they attend mass to sing religious songs and listen to sermons by the Orthodox priest, who speaks vaguely (because of the military censorship) about the atrocities of war. Life in the camp is dull. In the winter snow covers their positions, making them look gray and even duller. A change comes with spring which awakens in the soldiers their true feelings and dreams. It is Stoil who expresses them in the most forceful and touching manner. One night he wakes up and goes outside the dugout, where he is struck by a wonderfully refreshing smell — the smell of "warm and moist earth." This sign of oncoming spring markedly changes Stoil's behavior: he becomes restless, sends more letters to his family with instruc-tions on how to run the farm, and thinks frequently about it. But above all he considers it to be almost a sin that he — a healthy man — cannot till the soil, cannot give it what it needs right now when the time is right. When Stoil meets Lieutenant Varenov and the latter tells him that "we still have to wait a little bit and suffer" before the war is over, he replies: "True, we suffer, but the soil, Mr. Lieutenant, the soil does not wait. Look, it speaks." Apart from the fact that we encounter here one of the first and most beau-tiful examples of nature personification in Yovkov's prose, the above con-versation is important for another reason: it impels us to consider whether it reflects a dichotomy between the general meaning of Yovkov's war stories and his description of soldiers, as Karanfilov maintains. First of all, what of Varenov's reaction to Stoil's complaint? He does not scold him for his "philosophical" reflections, but rather reacts with understanding and sym-pathy. It is clear from Varenov's behavior that he shares Stoil's worries. On the other hand, Stoil and his friends never ask why they should be fighting. They accept the situation with patience, as Varenov advises them to do. Varenov and the soldiers are united in their attitude toward the war, in accepting it despite all the difficulties and sacrifices they must endure. When Stoil and his friends attend Mass, they experience a deep religious feeling of reconciliation with God, and they do not fear dying "for something great and dear."

This story reveals another remarkable, — perhaps the most important — characteristic of these soldiers: their unshakable sense of duty. They all regard their participation in the war as an obligation which they must discharge to the best of their ability. In this attitude they are again united with Varenov. They make not the slightest protest against their fate. And, as if to reaffirm this unity between officer and men, Yovkov ends the story with a dramatic twist. The military unit is moved to the front line, and Varenov is wounded in the first battle. Stoil carries him from the battle in his arms; but he too is hit and both die locked in a brotherly embrace.

This sense of duty, camaraderie and heroism so evident in Yovkov's soldiers links his war prose with Tolstoy's *Sevastopol Tales*. There, Russian soldiers display similar characteristics: composure, generosity, endurance, sense of duty. In their deeds they are motivated by the same "shy but deeply rooted feeling of love for the fatherland."[8] They are also fearless in the face of death. Unlike Vsevolod Garshin's heroes, Yovkov's protagonists will never pose the question "why do I kill others?" Killing is part of the soldiers' task, and therefore one does not experience a conflict between duty and conscience.

As far as the war is concerned, there exists a remarkable unity between the writer, his narrator, and his protagonists, be they officers or privates: they are all infused with patriotic emotion. In the story "Bulgarka" (Bulgarian Woman), Yovkov shows that women too, traditionally kept out of actual combat, can be useful in wartime, and even heroic in their deeds. When the enemy attacks a small town, "then both the old and the young, women and children come to the aid of their soldiers, in whatever way they can." The most effective aid, however, comes from Shina. She has learned that machine-guns when in constant use can become overheated. Herself tireless, encouraging others by her example, Shina spends all afternoon carrying water to cool the guns on the front line. Her effort is rewarded when the enemy is driven from the town.

Another story, "Balkan," describes a dog unusually attached to the place he used to guard. In his capacity as editor of *Demokraticheski pregled*, Elin Pelin, one of the foremost Bulgarian writers,[9] refused to publish this story on the grounds that he did not understand the role of the dog, Balkan. The dog is stationed at a military post on the Bulgarian-Romanian border. He regularly "inspects" the border to help Bulgarian soldiers catch smugglers. When war breaks out, the Bulgarians are forced to retreat. Initially Balkan leaves with them, but after a few days he returns to the outpost and "resumes" his duties — he starts to patrol the old border again.

This story may be read on two levels: realistic and symbolic. Whichever one we choose, the story reveals a twofold meaning. The return of Balkan may be interpreted as a literal expression of the simple attachment animals often show to places they have inhabited for some time. But there is an inherent deeper symbolic meaning too: the fact that the dog comes back to affirm the old border anew indicates that "our soldiers" will also return. For civilians, Balkan brings a ray of hope, from which we may conclude that even animals do not abandon the fight against injustice. This interpretation is buttressed by the fact that Balkan develops a new trait: a strong resentment of the Romanian soldiers.

The atmosphere of Yovkov's stories is one of firm opposition to the enemy; there is not a shadow of doubt on the part of those involved in the war as to the legitimacy of their cause. But it should be noted that this acceptance of war in Yovkov's early prose is not to be explained by patriotic motivations alone. When in "The Memorable Day" the declaration of war is met with a loud and spontaneous "hurrah" from the soldiers, this enthusiasm is caused not so much by patriotic feeling as by a personal sense of the mystique of war. This is particularly true of younger soldiers, who have not yet experienced direct confrontation with the enemy and the horrors of combat.

There is yet another thing which attracts soldiers to war: they treat it as an adventure, as something that releases them from daily boredom and brings them new friendships. Another South Slavic writer, and Yovkov's contemporary, touched upon exactly the same motif but presented it from a different ideological and artistic perspective. In *Hrvatski bog Mars* (The Croation God Mars), Miroslav Krleža shows that at the beginning of the war Croatian peasants were happy to be drafted and to leave their villages. They naively believed nothing could be worse than the condition of a laboring peasant, and are glad to get away from everyday chores. Soon, however, they realize their mistake: the war turns out to be a nightmare as short-term heroes become pitiful victims.

No such interpretation in possible with Yovkov, at least not for his stories written between 1913 and 1918. His soldiers remain faithful to the spirit of adventure; they must face death, which, of course, makes them pensive about the war; they envisage difficulties but never succumb to despair; in short, they face the horrors of war with dignity. Yovkov's soldiers are heroic even in defeat. Although the author of *The Harvester* depicts human suffering, he is basically opposed to the "mystical idealization of the philosophy of suffering,"[10] and remained so for the whole of his career. If the behavior of Krleža's peasants is to be explained by social and political motivations (war is unjust; since it is caused by aberrant social conditions, it leads to political radicalization, etc.), Yovkov's heroes embody moral and romantic idealism. Their moral dilemma is this: on the one hand, they are attached to the land, which needs to be cultivated; on the other, they know that, being soldiers, they must fight. However, they cope with this conflict extremely well: in the final analysis, the love of fatherland always prevails over personal feelings.

Romantic idealization is evident in the description of war as "poetry which stems from an epic cause," as a simple and at the same time almost esthetic experience. In his stories Yovkov avoids psychological analysis of characters. When he writes about death, he does so only in passing. This approach separates him from both Tolstoy and Garshin. The thought of death is, of course, always present in the soldier's mind, but only as a moment of uneasiness, as a short spurt of thought in a larger overall picture. In "Purvata pobeda" (The First Victory), amidst the general excitement and joy before the first encounter with the enemy, there is a latent apprehension of death:

> Deep down in the soul there still remained a corner where one felt the sharp pains of a hidden wound, where the specter of death knocked with the persistence of a belated wanderer and whispered: 'Do not forget me. I am here' ...[11]

But such fragments are rare. Yovkov's strength lies in his unusual ability to describe first, a great variety of episodes in war, and second, the mosaic of battle itself. Under the first category one can group stories which show the impact of war on the personal life and behavior of people, mainly civilians; their participation in or experience of war; the surprises of trench warfare, in which no mass movements of soldiers or large military detachments are involved. In the latter case, the narration resembles an anecdote with an unusual ending (e.g. "Treta smyana" [The Third Shift] or "Sreshtu Nova Godina" [On New Year's Eve]). In every case, the story is set in either a frontier village (or small town), or at a more or less stable front line, where soldiers are in the trenches.

III   THE EPISODES, OR WAR AS ANECDOTE

Personal tangles resulting from the course of war are given a romantic touch. Usually, they are presented as a kind of romance involving a girl and a young officer. In "Pesenta na Solveig" (The Song of Solveig), a talented violinist, Anya, falls in love with her former classmate, who is now an officer. Looking through the window shortly before a performance, Anya notices the silhouettes of three people walking along the street: an old woman, an old man and a young officer. After a while she recognizes the young man as her former classmate, and at the same time her neighbor from across the street, who used to tease her by playing the same pieces on the fiddle whenever she practiced hers, as a result of which he was given the nickname "violino secondo." Years have passed, Anya has pursued her career abroad; the officer has matured too, and now, with a scar on his face — a visible war wound — he looks like a true hero. This stirs Anya's imagination. In a few hours she undergoes an incredible emotional metamorphosis, just before her appearance on stage. From a girl known for her excellent technique on the violin but nothing else, Anya is transformed into an artist, an individual who plays with feeling and love. A critic who has followed her career closely is astounded: the cause of this change remains a mystery to the audience. In the final minutes of her performance Anya plays the song of Solveig[12] — symbol of love and fidelity.

A similar narrative and thematic scheme occurs in the story "Prustenut" (The Ring). A young officer, Arso Lambrev, is about to depart for a short leave to visit his fiancée. He wants to make her a gift of a ring. As he shops in a jewelry store, the owner of the store suggests that he should buy a golden ring with a small diamond so pure and so brilliant that it looks like a "divine tear." Suddenly Lambrev associates this metaphor with a real tear shed by a young woman, Mariya, whom he met while a prisoner of war and who helped him to survive his imprisonment. Since the town where this occurred was not far away, Lambrev decided to visit it on his way home. He finally succeeds in finding Mariya, and decides to give the gift to her. He visits his fiancée Vyara, empty-handed.

The plots of these stories are never dramatic, often simple, and sometimes border on sentimentality. Yovkov, however, could capture the most subtle nuances of human feelings without resorting to detailed "psychologization," that is, complicated and lengthy descriptions of the "human soul" and its experiences. The sudden transformation of feelings is related to a chain of exterior events. The author does not pretend to be a psychologist who knows everything about his protagonists; he offers insights into their thinking only rarely, confining himself to what he observes on the surface. This kind of "behaviorism" is a clear departure from Yovkov's early stories and a step closer to the compact, economical and simple prose of the 1920's.

In other stories — such as "Vodachkata" (The Guide-Woman), "Sedemte" (The Seven), "V stroya" (In Mounted Formation) and "Bulgarian

Woman" — the war helps to reveal traits of character that under normal circumstances would remain concealed. A shy and modest teacher, Vangeli, proves to be a bold woman who does not hesitate to guide soldiers to an important mountain pass. "In Mounted Formation" describes a horse which cannot get used to its dismissal from the military service; when the horse hears a march played during a military parade, it joins the nearest column side by side with the horse of the commanding officer.

In all these cases Yovkov develops a unidimensional protagonist (whether human or animal), a protagonist displaying heroism and devotion to a higher patriotic purpose.

Finally, "The Third Shift" and "On New Year's Eve" picture the war as a kind of game with an unexpected ending, as an anecdote with a comic turn of events. The beginning of the first story unfolds in a number of droll conversations between soldiers and their officer, Tsolov, who tries to inculcate in them the ideal of vigilance while they are on sentry duty. The clash between the simplistic logic of his explanation and the seriousness of his listeners produces humorous effects. When Petranov takes over the guard — "the third shift, or the time when anything can happen" — he remembers well Tsolov's remarks, and in particular one about a "moving mountain": Tsolov had warned them that a soldier on guard must watch even for a "moving mountain." And yet Petranov almost fails to give the alarm when the enemy approaches the trenches, because he takes the white uniforms of the enemy soldiers for patches of fog. However, the whole has a happy ending, and the soldiers remember the episode as a good joke.

A characteristic of these stories is their faithful rendering of the everyday wartime atmosphere. Despite surprises and even changes in the lives of people, they still participate in the ordinary flow of life, which is reflected also in the quiet and objectified (in most cases third person) narration.

IV   THE BATTLE, OR WAR AS ADVENTURE

The situation changes completely whenever Yovkov sets out to describe a battle. He has been called a master of battle description, and rightly so. In all such stories — "The Memorable Day," "Before Odrin," "The First Victory," "Kaypa," "On the Other Side" — the narration is more vivid because of the changing details of an unusual situation, and is also more subjective (as a rule the narration is in the first person). In these stories the adventurous nature of war emerges most strongly. Man is torn away from his usual environment, and confronted with danger in a new and unknown world.

This world is founded on the principle of collectivity and typified by mass movements. It would be, however, a simplification to assume that Yovkov limits himself to describing exchanges of fire, attack and counterattack, killing and all the other horrors of direct military confrontation. One can distinguish three major stages of battle: a deadly silence before the combat; the combat itself, usually the most vivid depiction of the story; and the aftermath. All three structural components do not necessarily enter into each story. "Before Odrin," for example, is almost entirely devoted to a description of the aftermath of battle.

A. THE SILENCE

The most impressive images of silence as a component of struggle occur in "Kaypa." Here, as the battle reaches its climax, Yovkov emphasizes the contrast of a sudden silence filled with tensions and emotions oscillating between hope and despair, between brief relief and renewed anxiety, between resignation and anger:

> All keep silent, nobody speaks because there is only one thought in everybody's mind, one feeling in everybody's soul: expectation. Because all are living through the last minutes of doomed victims. One awaits the final hour alone. And in this silent waiting under grenades and bullets, there is something similar to the motionless ferocity of a bull accepting barbs in the live flesh of its body.[13]

At the same time, however, these short intervals in the fighting bring soldiers closer together and strengthen their friendship. Each wants to touch the other because this gives them the illusion of greater security.

The silence is ordinarily of rather short duration; it precedes the battle, when everyone is keenly aware of the impending combat. In fact, it is probably the most painful moment of battle: one can hear "the beating of soldiers' hearts" as the tensions of uncertainty reach their climax. Sometimes nature provides a dramatic aura that exposes the ominous character of the silence, as, for example, in "Kaypa":

> A mute silence reigns over the foggy field and the uninhabited, abandoned village, the outline of which can be seen nearby. Everything as it were holds its breath, anxiously awaiting something. Only the monotonous and somnolent drumming of the rain can be heard.[14]

B. THE COMBAT

While silence in general allows Yovkov's heroes to ponder the nature of war and to apprehend it as something unusual in human life, the battle itself brings out exceptional characteristics of both men and war. Yovkov is particularly fascinated by human courage. As the narrator of "Kaypa" watches the soldiers on the attack, he makes the following comment: "Yes, they will win — and what selflessness, what fearless and proud defiance of death!"[15] This sort of sentiment emerges even more strongly in "The First Victory," as Second Lieutenant Randev leads his soldiers to the attack: "But what majestic beauty, what lofty dignity infuses every man who quietly and fearlessly goes to meet death itself!"[16] If contempt for death is the first quality of a magnificent man, sacrifice is the other. In Yovkov's battles there is no time for hesitation and no place for cowardice. Situations change in kaleidoscopic fashion; the course of battle is associated with noise, cries, bursting shells and — above all — with moving masses of people, be they soldiers or civilians, trying to escape the slaughter. In describing a battle Yovkov seldom concentrates his attention on characters as individuals, preferring instead to catch a glimpse of a person in a particular situation and then to refer to the same person on another occasion which contrasts starkly with the first. An instance of this in "The First Victory" is a young soldier whom the narrator meets at the railway station in Burgas as he is being seen off by his family, and some girls; later on, after a fierce battle, he sees the dead body of the same soldier. This contrastive presentation is typical of Yovkov's abbreviated, concise style of narration. It is also more dramatic. It makes a direct impression on the reader and helps him to grasp vividly the tragic nature of war.

Through all Yovkov's stories devoted to the war on the Turkish front ("The Memorable Day," "Before Odrin," "The First Victory," "Kaypa," "On the Other Side"), only two 'characters' appear more or less regularly in the course of the action: the narrator himself and Second Lieutenant Randev. Their appearance tells us something about the close friendship between these two officers, and at the same time lends a certain unity and continuity to these stories. Here Yovkov displays for the first time his inclination towards writing stories in a cycle devoted to a definite theme. He proceeds like a great painter, who, before putting his picture on canvas, makes sketches of the various fragments which will comprise the complete and final tableau. The main hero of such a work in Yovkov's case is the war itself, with the battle as its major component.

Whenever Yovkov describes a battle, he uses Homeric similes. It reminds him of hell. He compares it to a thunderstorm or hailstorm, or to both at once. When it rages at its peak, the narrator perceives it as something which runs counter not only to human nature but to nature in general. It evokes anxiety which spreads to animals and birds. Horses carrying ammunition shiver whenever they approach the front line. At one point the narrator watches a flight of birds approaching the battlefield. When they reach the site of the battle they are frightened by its din, fly higher up and turn back in the direction from which they came. And yet, at the same time the view of the battlefield is beautiful; it elicits admiration because it provides the real test of human dignity.

C. THE AFTERMATH

As a rule, the aftermath brings relief, joy over having survived another sinister danger, and again uncertainty about the future. It throws up details which constitute the inseparable attributes of a temporary ceasefire: corpses strewn over the field; their burial; the digging of trenches; an encounter with enemy patrols; the taking of prisoners; and so on. Aside from relaxing tensions, the aftermath as described in "Before Odrin" is suffused with an atmosphere of genuine concern for suffering and human compassion in its various facets. In one especially touching fragment the narrator speaks of the dead enemy soldiers. Looking at their scattered personal belongings — haversacks, socks, cups, shirts — he thinks that they were all packed by the loving hand of a mother, wife or sister who did their best to prepare them in the hope of their speedy return. And he comments: "Indeed, was it possible to regard these dead men as enemies? Indeed, was there any place for hatred, for vengeance?"[17]

In general, Yovkov's attitude towards the enemy is chivalrous, but it also depends on his nationality. Curiously enough, Yovkov is more generous towards the Turks, who oppressed Bulgaria for centuries, than toward Romanians or Serbs. Sometimes he seems especially biased against Romanians, presenting them as mean, petty, vengeful, malicious and cowardly. This attitude might be due to the fact that the Romanian assault against its southern neighbor in the Second Balkan War was a most unexpected and treacherous blow that shattered Bulgarian dreams and expectations.

The aftermath provides an outlet for psychological tension. The narrator calls it "a voiceless, uneasy pause," during which soldiers exchange "glances of hatred and moral enmity." They still cannot recover from the horrors of bloodshed, and everything around them appears to be suspicious, mysterious and hostile.

V IMPRESSIONISM OF THE WAR PROSE

The stories discussed thus far are distinct from the rest of Yovkov's war prose with regard to both content and form. To this point I have analyzed

some important aspects of their content. Now we may take a closer look at
the way these stories are constructed.

To understand their formal peculiarities, one must keep in mind that
Yovkov's narrator displays all the characteristics of an intellectual, a representative of the educated stratum of society, who is concerned mainly with
the artistic appreciation of reality. To be sure, his esthetic credo still
remains a Modernist one, as it was in his immature prose, but with a
noticeable shift from the Symbolist mannerism typical of the early poetry
and prose towards a vivid and colorful Impressionist style.

Yovkov's Impressionist prose has never been thoroughly examined.[18] The
lack of a precise theoretical definition of literary Impressionism does not
make such a task easier. M. E. Kronegger, for instance, suggests that one
may hardly speak of Impressionism in the sense of a literary trend, but
must rather treat individual Impressionist writers or elements of Impressionism in the works of some authors.[19] In discussing Impressionist artists,
M. E. Kronegger notes that "the keyboard of each impressionist artist
differs; there is nothing in common between Monet's cathedrals and
Cézanne's still lifes."[20] This statement is even more relevant when applied
to literature, so much do writers differ from one another in implementing
Impressionist principles in literature. And yet, despite all these differences,
one can still discover specific approaches typical of Impressionism in general. A trait common to all Impressionists is their sensitivity to language,
which manifests itself primarily in an emphasis on visual and sensory
aspects of narration. Reality cannot be grasped by intellectual analysis, but
only seized by direct and spontaneous observation. Consequently, language
is not understood as thought or concept, but as a vehicle to render sensa-
tion, to evoke sound images or colorful effects. The narrating subject must
merge, as it were, with external objects to create an impression of true
reality. Thus we arrive at the crucial principle of Impressionist esthetics: the
ultimate point of departure for each Impressionist artist, whether painter or
writer, is reality itself, though this reality is filtered through the prism of
highly subjective, personal experiences. This principle distinguishes Impressionism from Symbolism, the latter being concerned with the world that
lies far beyond ordinary, sensory human experience. While a Symbolist
turns his attention to the absolute, an Impressionist is attached to the real.

If we examine Yovkov from this point of view, then the Impressionism of
his war prose becomes obvious, and should be considered a step forward
toward the type of Realism which he attained in the 1920's and practiced
continuously in the 1930's. There is no doubt that Yovkov's war prose
constitutes a definite departure from the abstract and somewhat lifeless

Symbolism of his early writing. However, if we call this transition Impressionism, we should avoid oversimplification by reducing the characteristics of Yovkov's Impressionist style to an exceptional fascination with color and vivid depiction of events. Such an interpretation is tempting, and has actually been offered,[21] but it brings out only one aspect of the writer's Impressionism.

One should begin with something that has hitherto been overlooked but which, in my judgment, constitutes one of the most interesting features of Yovkov's narrative style. I refer to the technique of the moving camera eye as applied by the writer in some of his war stories. Yovkov constantly focuses on different aspects of both spiritual and material reality, constantly alters the narrator's angle of observation. In fact, his role is that of a cameraman who tries to catch in rapid sequence the changing events and various objects of a given situation. Thus, the flow of the narration speeds up to the maximum. One has the impression that the narrator wants to incorporate as many details as possible into his field of observation. However, as the eye of the camera constantly shifts from one object to another, from one event to another, from one action to another or from one reflection to another, the reality that emerges from such a presentation appears to be fragmented, and unfinished. It is integrated by a situation or underlying mood, as for example in such stories as "Kaypa," "The Memorable Day," "The First Victory," or "Svyatata nosht" (Easter).

According to some theoreticians, the characteristics discussed above are the most significant signs of literary Impressionism.[22] Where Yovkov's prose is concerned, those characteristics can sometimes be discovered within a single sentence. "Kaypa" contains the following example: "Yes, they will win — and what selflessness, what a fearless, and proud defiance of death!"[23] The first part of this grammatical unit constitutes a sober assessment that the Bulgarians will win. The elliptical second part — without any logical, cause-effect relationship to what has gone before — expresses admiration for the manly qualities of the soldiers. In fact, what is at work here is the Chekhovian device of incongruous dialogues between people speaking to each other in unrelated monologues. In Yovkov, this device is somewhat modified, for it occurs in this particular case within one sentence. There are not many such extreme examples as this one, but it does illustrate a certain artistic principle typical of Yovkov's Impressionist prose. His attention is constantly shifting — trying to include as many details and events as possible, while at the same time avoiding naturalistic description.

A clear application of this narrative technique is demonstrated in "Kaypa." The story starts with general thoughts about war, which puts unknown and small villages on the map because they are the sites of important battles. This introduction is followed by a description of the battle itself, but one which contains two levels. First it tells of the heroism of soldiers fighting in the front line and those waiting in reserve. As Yovkov puts it, some are "on the scene" and some remain "behind the scenes." He also includes a description of weather and field conditions — heavy rain and mud put men under greater pressure and make it more difficult for them to endure the horrors of war. The entire narration is sprinkled with small, seemingly unimportant details: the dead bodies of Bulgarian soldiers, the Turks retreating in chaos and disorder, encounters with officers, and so on. These details are complementary, and together form an all-encompassing picture of the battle. The whole depiction is overlaid by the very subjective impressions of the narrator, who observes objects and events in his own very peculiar way.

It is clear that Yovkov created his own mode of depicting war. He pictures great battle scenes which call to mind the monumental canvases of the Russian painters, Vasily Vereshchagin or Ilya Repin. It is no accident that Yovkov mentions these two artists in "Before Odrin" and compares their war paintings to what the narrator has seen as a soldier in the course of action. Moodiness, susceptibility to color, sound and dynamic movement — these are the principal characteristics of Yovkov's war prose. The mood of ghastly mystery typical of the early stories "Zvezdna vecher" (A Starlit Evening), "Elka," "Sorrow," recurs in considerably subdued form in such war stories as "Sluchayni gosti" (Fortuitous Guests), "Kray mesta" (In the Vicinity of Mesta), "Easter," "Before Odrin." It should be added that in comparison with the earlier stories in which moods of ghastliness and mystery predominate, the war stories contain a greater variety of moods, including solemnity, seriousness, and serenity.

In "Easter," a moonlit night before Easter moves Kuzev to lyrical outpourings about the years of his childhood. In "Fellow-Countrymen" a solemn mood dominates during Mass as soldiers and officers listen to Father Vurban's sermon. When Stoil speaks of land, he uses lofty and pathetic words. An interesting example of a similar mood can also be found in "Easter," when one hears on both sides of the front line the religious hymns sung by Greek and Bulgarian soldiers. In describing this, Yovkov introduces the word *penie* (singing). The idea of using this lexical archaism is very fertile, for it is always associated with the solemnity of religious ritual and so the reader is immediately made aware of the kind of music being sung. By careful use of linguistic means, without unnecessary descriptions, the writer achieves a remarkable plasticity of image and evokes the intended mood.

This tendency to create situations of somber mood is intricately linked to an almost obsessive sensitivity to colors, especially black. We can easily find in the war prose whole passages in which events or external natural phenomena are described exclusively in terms of color impressions. The movement of army units, battles, fields and roads are perceived as patches and lines of color. Whether such a reaction was the consequence of the author's psychological predispositions or the result of some definite literary convention is difficult to determine with any certainty. As we already know, Yovkov once toyed with the idea of entering a school of fine arts to study painting, but opted for a brief study of the law. One can find among Yovkov's manuscripts some drawings and sketches which testify that the plastic arts were not foreign to the author of "Fellow-Countrymen." What then becomes puzzling is the fact that this strong predilection for color disappeared entirely in Yovkov's writing after 1920. Consequently, one is inclined to believe that literary convention rather than a psychological factor played the decisive role in sustaining this feature of Yovkov's war prose. Among Symbolist poets in Bulgaria, there were several who, at one time or another in their literary activity, used color impressions as their main artistic device. One such poet is Khristo Yasenov:[24] the color effects of his early poems remind one very much of that in such Yovkov stories as "Fellow-Countrymen" and "Sreshtu Nova Godina" (On New Year's Eve).

Yovkov operates with three major colors: black, white and red; there is a striking lack of intermediary shades and semi-tones. However, if we were to translate to canvas the narrative flow of Yovkov's war prose according to the frequency of color choice, we would see that black prevails clearly over both red (second) and white (third). After them follow blue, green and so on. The first two colors (black and red) symbolize the horrors of war, while white is neutral. In most cases particular objects and phenomena are given constant color designations: a road is white; a human mass is black; fields and trees are green or sometimes yellow; the havoc of war and fires is red; animals are white. Moreover, Yovkov readily uses contrasts, such as black--white and red–black (the latter juxtaposition is the most frequent); and once a contrastive combination of colors assumes the form of an oxymoron: "red snow." The interplay of colors often creates enchanting, magnificently pyrotechnical visions, as for example: "This magical play of the stars was turning itself into a quiet and mysterious murmur";[25] or: "the searchlights from the fortress exposed to our eyes some strange and fairy-like sights."[26]

Sometimes Yovkov's colors form a queer mosaic, or remind the reader of a splendid embroidery:

> The valley below the camp is as beautiful as ever, there are still big bright blotches of flowers. It is as if there were spread out there a light-green silk fabric — fantastically embroidered in many hues.[27]

There is also noticeable in Yovkov a reverse tendency, a tendency to unify and reduce the richness of color tones and semi-tones into a single color — "grey and heavy." This happens usually at dusk. The nightfall and night not only unify colors, they also cause the contours of objects to dissolve into disorder. In Yovkov's war stories chaos is a synonym of blackness; and if there is any word the author misuses, it is "chaos." Whatever happens during the night or at dusk falls into chaos.

There is no need of more examples to illustrate this point, but it is necessary to note certain other devices typical of Yovkov's war prose. In order to set off the color black, Yovkov often shows objects, human silhouettes and animals from a distant perspective, placed against the background of a bright horizon or burning villages. Seen from a distance, objects lose their shape as we know them at short range. Watching from afar, we discern only vague outlines or mere dark spots. Yovkov often speaks of "black silhouettes" moving on the horizon: "Against the reddened sky, after sunset, one could see a black and seemingly unusually large silhouette of a dog."[28]

Sometimes, the author heightens the intensity of black by adding an epithet or by using a synonym in relation to something that has already been described as black. Thus we encounter quite often such phrases as "black darkness," "black crows," "black clouds" and so on. In the story "Triumph," Yovkov reinforces this by speaking of "pitch" blackness.

Especially interesting are those segments of the war prose in which Yovkov describes the surrounding reality (people, phenomena of nature, objects) mainly by distinguishing colors, dispensing with their other aspects. In the course of such description each subsequent component of reality is "marked" by a different color. Thus, a whole scale of colors is introduced in a relatively short fragment of text, creating something resembling a symphony of colors. This is particularly conspicuous in such stories as "The Memorable Day," "On the Other Side," "The Seven," "Mustapha Achi," and "Triumph." One example will illustrate this:

> The radiance of the fire fell upon this strange scene. One side of horses and people was brightly lit, the other was immersed in black shadows. The bright-blue mass of prisoners shone even stronger.[29]

Here, in three consecutive sentences there are four visual color effects: radiance, brightness, blackness and brilliant blue. Furthermore, the entire passage preceding this quotation is saturated with a great variety of colors as well. In the story "On New Year's Eve," an officer's boots at one point appear yellow, and at another — red. Since Yovkov prepared his texts for publication very carefully, it seems unlikely he overlooked this shift. This example illustrates Yovkov's sensitivity to colors very well.

Thus far we have dealt with the characteristics of Yovkov's prose which distinguish him from other prose writers who wrote about war. Neither the spare narration of Mikhail Kremen[30] nor the psychological realism of Vladimir Musakov[31] can be compared to the glamour of the battle scenes in Yovkov's prose. And indeed, his evocative moods and his extensive use of colors do not exhaust the stylistic devices he employed to reflect the fullness of impressions gathered by the author as participant in and observer of battles. Let us dwell for a moment on one of Yovkov's favorite devices in the war prose: contrast. The subject matter itself — war — lends itself perfectly to the application of contrast. This device permits the incorporation into one relatively short narrative of contrasting moods and situations encountered by soldiers in wartime. Yovkov demonstrates, in fact, an amazing inventiveness in creating contrasts. Aside from the white–black color contrast already mentioned, Yovkov seems very fond of contrasts of storm and calm, motion and stillness, the horrors of war and the beauty of nature. Whole stories are built upon this principle of opposition. The first part of "Fortuitous Guests" contains a gradual buildup of elements of danger: first, the reader learns that the sea is choppy; next, a storm rages over the sea; the climax is reached as the sea "roars," "the gale is furious," and the "waves growl." In the anticlimax the calm is restored as the sky clears and the sea ceases to be a dangerous element. At the end we read: "The sea was as calm and smooth as a sheet of congealed glass, and it glittered in the sunlight."[32]

Contrasts forming the framework of the major event (the arrival of a young couple at a military unit seeking shelter) are supplemented by the contrastive presentation of certain characters. While the young girl is presented as a personification of womanhood, beauty and goodness, the soldiers represent ruggedness, strength and virility.

As in "Fortuitous Guests" the storm yields to beautiful weather, so in "Mustapha Achi" the immobility of the troops is suddenly transformed into its opposite — dynamic movement. The cavalry regiments waiting for the command to attack *suddenly* (*izvednuzh*: italics mine, E. M.) charge and complete the task of annihilating the enemy. There exists an obvious analogy between the cavalry charge at Mustapha Achi and the scud of the cavalry unit in the "Beliyat eskadron" (White Squadron). In the latter, the transition from a static to a dynamic state occurs as suddenly as it does in "Mustapha Achi," but with one difference: the cavalry adds color effects — the galloping white horses create the impression of a moving white wall.

VI SYMBOLS

The symbol as a literary device plays an important role in Yovkov's war prose, and continues to do so in his later short stories, thus contributing to what has been called the "visionary realism" of his prose. However, it should be pointed out that the symbols in the war prose differ substantially from those in the writer's early stories. The latter are more abstract, vague and moody, while the former are distinguished by their concreteness. They express definite ideas or visions, and approach allegory.

In fact, a symbolic meaning may be discovered even in such stories as "The Song of Solveig" and "Bulgarian Woman." In the first, a song played by a young violinist, Anya, expresses her concealed love for a young officer and compassion for his parents. This symbol is also the key to all understanding of Anya's artistic metamorphosis. The second story may be regarded as a continuation of the Vazov tradition started in his novelette *Edna bulgarka* (A Bulgarian Woman), a story about a woman who helps those fighting against the Turkish yoke. Yovkov's Shina also embodies the best characteristics of the Bulgarian woman.

The author created a highly poetic symbol in the lyrical impressions of "In the Vicinity of Mesta." In the garret of an old house owned by a rich farmer, Khadzhi Ibrahim, the narrator finds many odds and ends, among which are a few strings of sheep-bells that in the past served both to decorate and locate sheep. Whenever Khadzhi Ibrahim touched these bells, each emitted a different tone. The narrator calls them "the most emphatic language of the past," and in the end he writes: "And in these silent sounds, under the dust of years was buried forever the charming poetry of the good old days."[33] In other words, the "silent sounds" symbolize the bygone days of the past. This story is also one of the first examples of Yovkov's attachment to the past and his cult of patriarchal tradition, so powerful in his later writings.

In the story "The Ring," a ring (usually a symbol of engagement or marriage) bought by Lieutenant Lambrev becomes a sign of gratitude and friendship for a girl who helped him to survive at a time of hardship.

Similarly, there is a symbolic connotation in "The White Squadron." The attack of the cavalry on white horses symbolizes the justice of the Bulgarian cause. The successful attack against the Romanians is a just retaliation for the sufferings inflicted on the Bulgarians through the treacherous aggression of their neighbors.

Yovkov reduced the role of symbols in the war prose. However, along with other means of artistic expression — the extensive use of colors, contrasts, the fragmentation of the narrative and its saturation with metaphors — symbols still contribute to the lyrical, impressionistic character of many of the war stories.

VII   PROTEST AGAINST THE WAR

Chronologically and artistically such stories as "Last Joy," "Khermina" and "The White Roses" belong to Yovkov's second period of artistic evolution, for "Last Joy" appeared in 1925, the other two in 1930. Thematically, however, they are still linked to the first, though this connection is of a peculiar kind. Before writing them, Yovkov thoroughly revised his attitude towards war, and began to condemn it with all the power of his artistic talent and moral indignation. Now war is depicted as a destructive force, one which thwarts the achievement of human happiness, and destroys whatever there may be of beauty between people. A tone of tragedy creeps into these stories, especially "Last Joy."

This long short story describes the life and death of its main protagonist — Lyutskan, the only flower vendor in a small provincial town. The author introduces him to the reader as follows:

> There was something very original, half-funny and half-serious, about the character and figure of Lyutskan, a figure so well-known to both young and old. This soft and simple-hearted man was capable of one mood only: a kind of exalted reverie, a kind of calm and self-satisfied bliss for which there was no visible reason.[34]

Lyutskan is indeed a joyful and good-hearted man. He lives in a small, remote town, making people happy by selling flowers; and he is, indeed, a generous vendor, especially with girls, to whom he gives more flowers than they can pay for. His business suffers severely from this, but he does not mind as long as he can please others. He has investigated the symbolism of flowers, and says each variety signifies something special: hyacinth means joy flowing from the depths of the heart; field daisies symbolize cordial simplicity (when selling daisies, Lyutskan would always add: "my love is pure"); violets represent latent love; carnations — chastity; narcissuses reflect calmness of feeling.

Lyutskan spreads joy through flowers. He considers himself to be a poet and tender lover. But in his urban environment he is treated with ironic forebearance — people see in him an eccentric, a comic figure deserving of pity. At the same time, people show him a great deal of friendliness because they know that the town would not be the same without Lyutskan, that romantic dreamer who enjoys, and is protected by, the idyllic atmosphere of the town. But the idyll ends abruptly with the outbreak of war. A modern Don Quixote and representative of the "good old days," Lyutskan is suddenly confronted with the most brutal realities of life, as he is drafted. He is enthusiastic, and proud to wear the uniform because it makes him feel important. He thinks of himself as a kind of modern knight. In his naiveté he does not even suspect what tragic consequences this change of life may portend.

As a soldier, Lyutskan does not lose his love for flowers, but this passion stands in crying contrast to the barbarity of war. It is interesting to compare the outer framework of action in Yovkov's earlier war stories with that of the "Last Joy." In the earlier stories the war is often pictured along with beautiful weather, sunshine, blue sky, and so on, but not in "Last Joy." Lyutskan's detachment is constantly exposed to rain, cold, cholera and clinging mud. The behavior of the soldiers is also different. In this regard "Last Joy" could best be compared with "Fellow-Countrymen," for both stories contain scenes about the collective life of soldiers over a longer period of time. And again, if in "Fellow-Countrymen" an almost pastoral harmony reigns, in the "Last Joy" Lytuskan's detachment is torn by inner conflicts and uncontrollable anger caused by a lack of food. For the first time Yovkov speaks of hunger and its effects on soldiers: it brings out hatred. The wheels of the war machine drag Lyutskan inevitably into its mechanism, and in the face of such brutality he is helpless. His love of flowers provokes violence or laughter, and both are devastating. When at one point a soldier grabs a white chrysanthemum from him, throws it to the ground and "begins ruthlessly trampling it with his boots," Lyutskan responds only with tears.

Eventually the protagonist is wounded, and dies a long, lingering death. The description of his agony is among the most moving scenes in Yovkov. The ending seems to suggest that Lyutskan's tragedy is twofold: he was as misunderstood in life as he was in death. When a colonel views Lyutskan's dead body, with its arms stretched towards a flower, he makes the following comment: "Look at his face, look at his outstretched arms. If he could have raised himself, he would have run to attack the enemy again."[35] The reader is well aware, however, the Lyutskan's "outstretched arms" do not signify that. In his last conscious moment, Lyutskan wanted to grasp the passion of his life — flowers growing just beyond the spot where he lay dying. He is no hero, but a victim of war.

Similarly, the unburied bodies of soldiers and human skeletons seen by the narrator in "Khermina" remind us of the cruelty of war, which ravages villages and towns. Dogs turned wild, roaming through the fields and eagles flying in the skies are the only living creatures; but they feed on human flesh.

Yovkov enters an even stronger human protest against the war in "The White Roses." A young officer's death puts an end to Angelina's love, leaving her plunged in deep mourning. Spas, a soldier who knows the true dimensions of Angelina's tragedy, asks the question: "Why must a terrible misfortune befall this good girl? Why, asked Spas, why?" Never before had any of Yovkov's protagonists formulated such a question. There is a "wound in Spas' soul": his disenchantment with the war and the pain this causes grow to the point where he becomes physically ill.

There is a great gulf between the stories glorifying war and those which condemn it unequivocally. Yovkov rid himself both of his early illusion that war may be considered a "just fulfillment of duties to the fatherland" and of his esthetic approach to it. Yovkov's war prose remains one of the first and clearest indications of the double nature of his narrative technique: the "official" narrator who regarded war as simple work, or duty to be fulfilled with honor, disappears after 1920.

The honesty of Yovkov's artistic evolution is also a measure of his greatness as a writer. Once he realized the fallacy of his former position, he revised it without hesitation. However, his later war stories ought not to be regarded merely as a kind of polemic with himself. In writing them he also challenged certain official ideals, illusions which turned out to be so out of touch with reality that they brought calamity upon the nation. Yovkov abandons the position of a writer who interprets the war theme on the basis of national myths to that of an artist concerned with the universal motives of war. The tragedy of Lyutskan and Angelina's sufferings will always be more understandable to people of all times and places than descriptions of battles, no matter how vivid. Thus Yovkov succeeded in showing the complex nature of war and its multidimensional aspects. Neither before nor after him has any other Bulgarian writer risen to such a level.

CHAPTER 3

The Recovered Tradition: The Prose Of The Twenties

Critics and historians of Bulgarian literature tend to treat Yovkov's prose as an artistically homogenous entity. As a result, in most cases, they adopt a rather static approach to the writer's literary legacy. Such an analysis is, no doubt, justifiable. There is a feature that underlies the whole of Yovkov's writing, lending to it a particular kind of unity which is recognizable at first sight in both his early and late artistic output. This characteristic has been aptly defined by Charles A. Moser as "visionary realism,"[1] a sort of romantic trait that permeates the whole of Yovkov's essentially realistic literary style.[2] The term is close to what is known in German literary criticism as "romantic realism,"[3] which has been used in relation to great writers who evade easy classification, such as Dostoevsky.

Though I accept this evaluation as basically correct, I would like to modify it slightly. It is true that Yovkov entered literature as a mature and very accomplished writer, who had quickly mastered the secrets of literary craft. This does not mean, however, that his work underwent no creative evolution. To put it another way, Yovkov's visionary realism at its inception differs from what it became in his more mature work of the 1920's and 1930's. A more dynamic approach to Yovkov's writing compels one to treat it as a process or, more precisely, as a continuing search for perfection. Those thoroughly acquainted with the writer's works will find in them support for this view.

Yovkov's early creative method in prose was shaped under the strong influence of Bulgarian Individualism and Symbolism (Neo-Romanticism). One can perceive this in the writer's inclination towards psychological prose over the years 1910–1913, and in the impressionistic, metaphorical style of his war stories (1914–1920). What is common to both these subperiods is the outlook of an intellectual who clearly identifies himself with certain esthetic, political, and ethical ideas of his time prevalent among the educated strata of society called the intelligentsia,[4] whose perception of social, national and human problems in particular is more sophisticated than that of other social strata. I have discussed briefly in Chapter One, and at some length in Chapter Two, the major characteristics of Yovkov's vision of the world as presented in the works of his first period. I will now consider the transitional years and Yovkov's second period of creativity, when he adopted values different from those he promoted in the first period.

Somewhere around 1920, Yovkov's world outlook begins to show signs of what might be called the wisdom of a *naroden* observer. The Bulgarian word *naroden* has a twofold meaning: it means "national," but at the same time it may be defined as a social class concept because it can refer to something with "simpleminded" or "peasant-like" characteristics, and may imply a world view based on the peasant cult of popular patriarchal tradition and folklore. Yovkov seems to have accepted the latter. The first manifestation of this attitude may be discovered as far back as a series of *feuilletons* entitled *Letopis 1912–1918* (Chronicles 1912–1918), published in various journals between 1914 and 1917. The *Chronicles* make an interesting appendix to the war prose, and bear witness to Yovkov's increasing interest in the peasants' philosophy of life and their patriarchal past. It is a kind of self-polemic with his own war stories, an escape from the harsh realities of the day. Later on, shortly before his death, Yovkov chose a different title for these chronicles: they were reprinted in 1937 as *Te pobedikha* (They Overcame), a title borrowed from a feuilleton of 1914. The inspiration for his piece came from a sculpture which Yovkov saw in 1913 at a Sofia art exhibition, the work of a young (and later very famous) Bulgarian sculptor Ivan Lazarov (1889–1953). The sculpture depicted a peasant with a rifle in his hands, walking beside an ox. The simplicity of this figure was truly striking. It embodied the very essence and spirit of Bulgarian national mythology by reflecting the importance of these two beings for the welfare of the nation. In Bulgarian popular tradition the ox was treated almost as a member of the family, "as a friend for an entire life," closely associated with the peasants' toil. Together, ox and peasant produce food and nurture people. They are, therefore, the mainstay of the nation. The war also revealed another characteristic of the peasant: his fearless patriotism and attachment to the land. These virtues are precisely the ones Yovkov cherishes most and brings to the attention of his readers in the feuilleton "They Overcame." Nor is this an isolated example. In other items, such as "Posledni rimlyani" (Last Romans) and "Dobrudzha nyakogo" (Dobrudzha in the Past), he praises the unity between man and nature that existed in the past by idealizing the past itself, for then, he says, "people loved their earth more strongly, more sincerely, more deeply" than now.

The realism of Yovkov's creative perception of life resulted in the emergence of two types of narrators in his prose, characteristic, respectively, of the early period and of the decades of the 1920's and 1930's. This can be demonstrated by juxtaposing the treatment of the peasant theme in the early stories with that found in the later periods. Although most of Yovkov's protagonists in his early prose are villagers, he does not approach them from the viewpoint of a *naroden* narrator. Except in "A Shepherd's Plaint,"[5] the narrator looks at rural life through the eye of a sophisticated intellectual — a psychologist or philosopher. The shift from intellectual to *naroden* narrator is accompanied by a depiction of people from the perspective of rustic wisdom. A similar shift occurs in the war prose: an "official" narrator in the early stories relates events of the war as a job to be done with honor. This attitude changed in a few stories written in the later period, when the narrator disapproves of the war: then he discerns its horrors and protests over the sufferings of simple people, such as soldiers and their relatives or friends.

The evolution taken by Yovkov's narrative subject is characterized by a gradual departure from the influence of Individualism and Symbolist poetics (or Neo-Romanticism, generally speaking) and the search for his unique artistic vision. Still, his search for new forms and essence of content could not have been fulfilled without the existence of some different literary tradition. It seems that Yovkov made a clear choice: he abandoned the Neo-Romantic current in literature for the spontaneous folkloristic and popular tradition, borrowing from it not only its means of artistic expression but also its vision of reality. The Neo-Romantic and folkloristic traditions share a common feature: they tend to idealize reality. To be sure, this idealization means something different in each tradition. The former inclines to perceive the world around us through the prism of individualistic, often pessimistic, even decadent dreams; the latter is based on the mythology of folklore and a cult of the past. Despite these differences, both traditions could include Yovkov as "visionary realist."

This central characteristic of Yovkov's literary method has been described by Moser as follows:

> It should therefore be plain that Yovkov was not the sort of "realist" who wished, at whatever cost to his personal illusions, to view unadorned the reality of contemporary life. In the final accounting, his literary method was based upon realistic description of a non-immediate vision of reality, a vision engendered by memory or imagination, usually grounded in personally experienced events of the *relatively distant past*. [Italics mine — E. M.] If there was a chance of present reality conflicting with his visionary reality, Yovkov consciously and knowingly rejected present reality, insofar as that lay within his power. Yovkov was a realist of highly idealistic stamp.[6]

We should, however, bear in mind the fact that after 1920 this "idealistic stamp" was clearly defined by Yovkov's acceptance of the patriarchal and popular tradition of the Bulgarian peasantry. He looked upon conflicts and their resolutions, ethics, charity and hatred, crime and punishment, essentially from the viewpoint of a popular narrator.

Yovkov himself revealed a surprisingly mature theoretical awareness at one point in a conversation with his friend and collocutor Spiridon Kazandzhiev, when he brought up the question of world outlook in a writer's attitude towards reality (in fact, he anticipated Gyorgy Lukács' thoughts on the same subject by more than twenty years). The conversation concerned another writer on peasant themes, the novelist Konstantin Petkanov. What he had to say of him can also be taken as Yovkov's artistic credo:

> It seems to me that I have well understood this writer because he moves within the confines of peasant life. There is something sound in him. One can see that he comes from the village, that he observed people and their life there, that he loves them; he has a firm relation to them; and he does not lack talent. And yet in spite of all this, he remains in his presentation of village life a member of the intelligentsia, a man of letters, a scribe. He does not proceed "from inside outward," but in reverse, "from outside inward"; I would even say from "outside" only. Therefore, he stops somehow on the surface, at visual representation — he does not touch the depth of man. And because of that he is not sufficiently truthful: the man perceives the village the way it is imagined by a member of the intelligentsia and [Petkanov] does not feel it as a world from which a member of the intelligentsia is cut off. For this reason he lacks proportion: i.e., what it is possible or not possible to say about the peasant and the village. The sense of proportion is missing because he does not depict "from within." Because of this lack of proportion he also lacks genuine poetry and genuine artistic language.[7]

The above quotation takes us to the heart of the matter where Yovkov's esthetics is concerned. From the time he began to think seriously about becoming a writer, he strove to become, in effect, a popular narrator who depicts "from within." In the perspective of Yovkov's biography this may be viewed as quite a natural development.

In a conversation with Kazandzhiev, Yovkov once made the following remark:

> I have not written a single work which is not based on real experience. I have a good memory, I remember everything. I relate almost every motif to the landscape I am familiar with, to the environment I lived in and which I know.[8]

On another occasion he supplemented this statement with an even stronger one:

> I lived in the provinces for thirty years. My character was formed during this time; from that time as well date all my endeavors and observations — the entire world in which I live. I am in contact with this world as far as my literary work is concerned too, and I think that I am right about all this.[9]

In other words, Yovkov leaves no doubts as to what has determined his vision of the world. At the same time, however, he makes it clear that the "real" world cannot be equated with the world of his fiction, and that moreover, an artist does not necessarily require the "real" world in order to create a successful literary work. Perhaps a painter should gather as many impressions as possible, but

> For a writer ... this is not absolutely necessary. It's more important to know what he is doing when sitting in a coffeehouse, for instance — is his spirit busy, or is he drowsing. This constant "contact" with life, this "reflection" of life in his works ... and so forth — all this I don't consider as necessary as people usually think.[10]

It should be noted that the narrator in Yovkov's works cannot be entirely identified with the writer himself. There is a distance between the author and his narrator. This may be shown through an examination of the motif of "sinful love" or "sinful beauty" in such stories as "Postolovi vodenitsi" (Postol's Mills) or "Albena," a concept which does not harmonize with the patriarchal norms of the love relationship. This motif seems to serve a twofold purpose: it reflects the author's own admiration for beauty, a theme which runs through the whole of his work; and second, its presence within the patriarchal world prevents these and other stories from becoming "sentimental" pastorals. It adds to the credibility of the narration. A subtly marked tension between the author and his narrator is constantly present, and this also explains why the narrator is not merely a naive, rustic observer, but rather someone who distinguishes clearly between good and evil, who promotes love of one's neighbor and understanding in accordance with patriarchal tradition, which, in its turn, coincides to a great extent with Yovkov's own set of moral values and idealistic visionary perception of reality.

As he continued to develop his thoughts on the relationship between art and reality, Yovkov remarked:

> Art is something different; it has its own means and its own ends; it should give a special joy — no matter what it depicts. This joy does not come from either the nature or the topicality of the theme or from the problem of a literary work of art. I think it depends on the character, taste and so forth of an artist, whether or not he is preoccupied with the present or the past.[11]

Yovkov's remark that "art should give joy" defines fully the extent of his creative evolution from Symbolist pessimism to the situation of a *naroden* narrator who sees the world in basically hopeful terms.

This transition to a new artistic position is manifested in two literary texts: in the novella "Mechtatel" (The Dreamer) and *The Harvester*, both published in 1920. While the former may be interpreted as a rejection of his previous world perception determined by neo-Symbolist esthetics, the second foreshadows his evolution toward a new narrative approach embodying an acceptance of the patriarchal past.

I "THE DREAMER"

The protagonist of "The Dreamer," Boyanov, is a post-office functionary in a small border town in Dobrudzha. He fills his life with dreams of achieving personal happiness with a wife and a family, since he lives at a remote border station, where he experiences an acute sense of isolation from the world at large. This feeling is reinforced by his constant encounters with travellers passing through to various destinations abroad.[12]

"The Dreamer" has received remarkably onesided interpretations from Bulgarian critics and literary historians. Critics discuss it quite often, but without going beyond viewing it as a simple reflection of tedious life in the provinces or, at best, as an expression of Boyanov's pathological love for Vyara Lozeva, a young traveller who passes through his post. Among Yovkov scholars only Professor Moser, in his article on Yovkov's visionary realism and the importance of daydreams in his prose, has fully defined the importance of this story.

A few additional remarks, however, will clarify certain points connected with this story. When analyzed from the perspective of Yovkov's creative evolution, "The Dreamer" gains in stature. It cannot be reduced to a simple manifestation of the relationship between reality and literature; that is, it cannot be interpreted as merely the "reflection" of real, material life. It must be read on more than one level. If it is, the question of Boyanov's daydreams becomes one of crucial importance, for we realize that, unlike dreams in certain other works of Yovkov's, Boyanov's daydreams are self-centered and self-destructive. To be sure, they are evoked by real conditions; but once set in motion they acquire a self-perpetuating and self-reinforcing power: they roll like an avalanche. Boyanov's daydreams are at one and the same time a solace and a torment. They have no positive effect on his personality, but rather, in the final analysis, bring about his annihilation. In this respect, "The Dreamer" is an isolated instance in the body of Yovkov's writing. After 1920 none of Yovkov's major heroes pursues a phantom for the sake of his own satisfaction.

Boyanov is preoccupied with his own inner world, with his own unhappiness, which makes it tempting to assume that Yovkov wanted to discredit a certain type of dreamer only, a dreamer motivated by an empty neo-Romantic loftiness. Dreaming, for instance, was not only a feature of Symbolist poetry, it was also quite fashionable among Symbolist poets. It drove some of them to death, for example the poets Ivan Boyadzhiev and later Peyo Yavorov. Yovkov's reservations about this kind of individualistic, selfish attitude emerge in the clearly ironic distance taken by the narrator towards his protagonist. Consequently, if analyzed within the parameters of Yovkov's creative evolution, this story may be treated as a literary document *par excellence*, as a sort of polemic with Modernist esthetics and literary stereotypes, and a farewell to the writer's own artistic past. "The Dreamer" rejects the individualistic, isolated dreamer in favor of another dreamer, one of the future, who cherishes his dreams for the benefit of others and wants to bring happiness to others. This is a permanent characteristic of all Yovkov's dreamers after 1920, including Lyutskan ("Last Joy"). Though the latter has been compared with Boyanov,[13] the comparison will not hold. Lyutskan found his main joy in selling flowers and his enchantment with them, not in obsession with his own feelings. Lyutskan is crushed not by his self-perpetuating dreams, but through a confrontation with the cruel reality of war. The narrator unquestionably sides with him.

II *THE HARVESTER*

In the final analysis Yovkov's "dreamer" considers himself unhappy because he does not enjoy the privilege of living in the city. He dreams of becoming the Minister of Telegraphs and marrying an attractive young wife. In short, he suffers from vanity. Thus, the narrator indirectly defines his position by depicting a species of negative hero who spurns the values of simple life in the provinces, and who suffers the inevitable consequences of such an attitude. Now Yovkov had to create a character who would represent directly the values which the narrator holds, and for sound and positive reasons. That new hero is Grozdan, the protagonist of *The Harvester.*

The Harvester is the first of Yovkov 's works to confirm his transition to a new artistic approach to reality. Apart from a few short stories written before the war, this work is also the first one set entirely in a village. But in this case there is no rift or distance to be felt between the narrator and the main idea of the novella. In fact, the narrator clearly promotes certain basic components of the peasant world view, and specifically the cult of industriousness and religious belief.

The plot of the story revolves around a conflict between Vulchan, a rich landowner, and Grozdan, a poor peasant. The animosity between the two is of long standing. Vulchan tries to organize a kind of rural association to promote cooperation among peasants and the use of agricultural machinery. He succeeds in persuading the peasants to buy a threshing machine for shared use in Lyulyakovo, the site of the action. To the best of my knowledge, Yovkov's description of the machine's arrival in Lyulyakovo is among the earliest literary passages reflecting the penetration of modern technology into the Bulgarian village.

Grozdan, however, who is influenced by a radical young teacher, Radulov, does not believe in the sincerity of Vulchan's efforts. He is convinced that under the leadership of Vulchan, a rich man, such an association cannot work to the benefit of the poor. During a quarrel which erupts between some peasants and Vulchan in the local inn, Vulchan is accused of exploiting his farm workers. The argument becomes particularly heated when the two arch-enemies confront each other: Vulchan calls Grozdan a drunkard, and Grozdan strikes Vulchan in the face.

From this point on the story takes a sharp turn. Vulchan brings his adversary to court, accusing him not of assault, but of unlawful ownership of a piece of land which supposedly belonged in the past to his family. In fact, the land had always been the property of Grozdan's father, Dobri, but had been mistakenly registered in Vulchan's name. Since both men were close friends, Vulchan had never paid any attention to the document, and even wanted to destroy it. Now, with the renewed hostility between him and Grozdan (Dobri is already dead), Vulchan decides to make use of the document to claim ownership of the land. The plan is well devised: the loss of this property means complete poverty and economic disaster for Grozdan. The latter is aware of the danger; he perceives Vulchan's treachery in the suit over a crime never committed, and this contributes to his own moral degeneration. He takes to drink, turns thief, and is suspected of arson in the burning of Vulchan's farm buildings. Grozdan neglects his own farm because he is so seized with hatred that he gives all his attention to the court case. Is there any way out of this spiritual crisis?

To answer this question we must discuss briefly a secondary plot which parallels the development of the central conflict. Suddenly in Lyulyakovo there arrives an old man, Nedko by name. Nedko is a self-educated artist who has in the past painted many icons for neighboring churches. But now he too is in moral decline — he is ailing, rarely sober, and lacks all zeal for work. Lyulyakovo's old priest, Stefan, helps Nedko by encouraging him to resume his vocation as icon-painter. Stefan tells Nedko there is someone who would like to buy an icon and offer it to the local church: that person is Vulchan, who wants to demonstrate his piety. Nedko decides to try painting again, and creates a beautiful icon which is different from anything he has painted before. It pictures Jesus Christ walking among fields of ripe grain and blessing the fruits of people's toil. The icon is installed in the church, and Vulchan adds a golden crown to it.

At this point Grozdan's story and Vulchan's intersect again. Grozdan becomes more and more immersed in crime. Learning that there is a golden crown over the icon, he and his friend Tachkata decide to steal it. Once this is done, however, he suffers unbearable remorse: committing sacrilege is more than Grozdan's conscience can endure. His peace of mind is shattered. From this time on Grozdan searches for spiritual rebirth and reconciliation with his enemies. An opportunity presents itself unexpectedly quickly: while walking one day along the fields Grozdan sees a fast-moving carriage pulled by runaway horses. It is clear that if they are not stopped the driver will be killed. Grozdan does not hesitate to help: at the risk of his own life he succeeds in stopping the carriage. It turns out he has saved the life of his arch-enemy, Vulchan. After this both Grozdan and Vulchan bury their animosity. The latter falls ill, and on his deathbed confesses that the land he took away from Grozdan was not his. He asks his sons to give it back to its rightful owner. Grozdan, on the other hand, has come to understand his own wrongdoing. Realizing that hatred is a destructive force which could bring complete disaster to him and his family, Grozdan follows the Christian principle of love of neighbor. He resumes his usual everyday work as farmer, and regains peace of mind.

The Harvester begins as an almost exemplary class-struggle story, but ends in a spirit of Christian reconciliation. Critics have pointed to Yovkov's dependence here on Leo Tolstoy.[14] Indeed, the author of *Resurrection* had astonishing numbers of followers in Bulgaria, in both the social and cultural realms. For example, communes were organized in Bulgaria on the basis of his theories. It is not, however, this aspect of Tolstoy's thought which most interested Yovkov.[15] Generally speaking, the Bulgarian writer was influenced mainly by Tolstoy's literary technique, by his introverted concern for man. More particularly, in *The Harvester* he tried to project into reality the unorthodox Christian code of moral behavior developed by the Russian master. The central conflict in *The Harvester* is resolved in accordance with Tolstoy's principle of "non-resistance to evil by force."[16]

The religious element is emphasized throughout the novel. Before painting his icon, Nedko has a vision of Jesus Christ walking in the fields, and, as he confesses to Father Stefan, he decides to commit it to canvas. After stealing the "crown," Grozdan is haunted by the image of Christ in the icon. It seems to him that he has in reality seen the Saviour walking through the fields as depicted on the canvas. This vision is interwoven with the image of Grozdan's late father, who admonishes his son for his having committed a "great sin." In fact, Grozdan's spiritual revival and his close reflections about God began with a dream which has a healing effect on his personality, giving vent to his frustrations and fears, and allowing him to realize that he has been led astray. From that moment he is on the road to spiritual recovery.[17]

Grozdan's troubles, however, are not caused merely by a weakening of religious feeling. He has also failed in fulfilling his duty as a tiller of the soil. And that is the real source of Grozdan's gradual decline. Once he went to court with Vulchan he lost his zeal for work and neglected his duties, and this has a disastrous impact on his personality. The motif of work emerges both in the first part of the novel and in its final chapters, when Grozdan recognizes the beneficent nature of toil. Thus Yovkov accentuates the importance of two elements essential to human happiness and harmony of life: religious faith and work.

The motif of work becomes a dominant theme in the story "Pesenta na koleletata" (The Song of the Wheels), first published in 1925 and a year later reprinted in the collection *Last Joy* (the second edition of this collection bore the title *The Song of the Wheels*). "The Song of the Wheels" "presents a master cartmaker who has devised a method of arranging pieces of metal on the axles of the carts he manufactures so that they will produce a pleasant musical sound as they move."[18] Each of these carts emits a different sound, a different refrain. Sali Yashar, the cartmaker, is not a simple artisan; he is a true artist in his trade. And yet he still dreams of creating something of more lasting value, something that would benefit people more than his carts. He thinks of building a well that would provide water for thirsty people, a bridge, or an inn that would give travellers a place of rest. In short, Sali Yashar is motivated by a noble urge to do good. He has more money than others, and wants to share it for the common weal.

One day, Sali Yashar hears the sound of a cart approaching, and recognizes the cart of his daughter Shakire, who has come to visit. At another point Dzhapar, the village watchman, tells Sali Yashar how he recognizes the carts of various people. After these events the old cartmaker realizes that he can make his best contribution by building carts.

> 'Allah!' — he whispered and struck his forehead. 'I have been blind, I have been stupid! What wells and what bridges do I want to build? Good works! Is there any work better than the one I am doing? Carts, carts, that's what I have to do.'[19]

His carts bring joy to people, and this is what God wants him to do. Sali Yashar offers money to Dzhapar, suggesting that he buy land to start farming. However, he no longer considers charity the most important goal of his life. What really matters is the building of carts: they are the work of his hands, and the most precious gift he can offer to others. They also give him satisfaction and peace of mind.

There is yet another aspect to the story worth noting here. Shakire, Sali Yashar's daughter, belongs to a whole gallery of women whom Yovkov created in the second period of his literary evolution.[20] Her distinctive feature is beauty, which softens the general roughness of life. There emanates from her an unusual charm which rejuvenates Sali Yashar, and inspires him to noble acts. "No," — thinks Sali Yashar — "God can lavish many things on a person, but there is no more precious gift than the gift of beauty."[21] At the same time, Shakire evades anybody's control, remaining master of her own destiny and indeed exercising invisible power over men. Dzhapar wanted to marry her when they were both young, but she rejected his proposal because it did not fit in with her marital plans. At the end of the story, we learn that Shakire's husband has died, and that she has accepted Dzhapar. Her domineering and to some extent even artful personality prevails again.

Yovkov described the captivating power women hold over men for the first time in the story "Sud" (1921; The Trial, also included in the collection *Last Joy*). The words he uses to characterize this type of woman are "beautiful," "imperious," "strong." The main character in the story, an old Turk named Tokmakchiyata, must appear in court to testify about a balk dividing the fields of two peasants, Kutsiya and Andrey, as well as delineating the border between two villages. Tokmakchiyata is one of the few men who knows the truth about it, and that truth does not favor Andrey. But even if it did, there could be little probability that Tokmakchiyata might testify on Andrey's behalf. Rumor has it that in the past Andrey killed Tokmakchiyata's son, Rustem. An unpredictable turn of events, however, alters the seemingly predictable outcome of the trial. In his youth Tokmakchiyata was in love with a woman named Mariya, by now long since dead. However, when Tokmakchiyata arrives at the place of the trial to indicate the true line of the balk, he notices a young woman who is not only beautiful but strikingly resembles Mariya. He realizes that she must be the daughter of his old love, and learns that she is Andrey's wife. Past memories and passions quickly revive and turn out to be stronger than rational considerations. When Tokmakchiyata is asked to identify the true boundary, he follows the false line, testifying against the truth and in favor of Andrey. Moreover, his old and dying friend, Saafet-Mola, does the same. Neither man can rid himself of the old spell of Mariya's beauty, vividly reincarnated in the person of her daughter. Feminine beauty incites irrational reactions, causing men to break ethical codes of behavior. Throughout his entire literary career, Yovkov emphasized the beauty of women. Sometimes this beauty releases destructive forces; sometimes it inspires noble acts in a constructive way. But in any case the author never condemns the passion for beauty. It provides the only justification Yovkov ever offers for human misbehavior or even crime.

III *BALKAN LEGENDS*

Balkan Legends, a cycle of stories published in 1927, belongs to the most typical manifestations of Yovkov's "visionary realism," and at the same time represents the most significant achievement of his literary career. Unlike his other works based on Dobrudzhan motifs, *Balkan Legends* grew out of Yovkov's love for the mountain region of his native Zheravna. It took him several years to write these stories. The first "legend," "The Shepherd's Plaint," appeared in 1910; the remaining nine were finished between 1922 and 1927, that is, during Yovkov's sojourn in Bucharest.[22] While working on this volume Yovkov made a meticulous collection of material such as folksongs and some debates on the historical past of Zheravna. In a letter written to Danail Konstantinov, a teacher from Zheravna, Yovkov wrote the following:

> To complete it [*Balkan Legends*] I need some materials from Zheravna — folksongs, popular beliefs, historical events, legends and so on. I have long wanted to visit Zheravna and look for what I need, but I can see that I shall not be able to do so, and I am forced to turn to you. I hope you will be so kind as to do me this favor .... Any and all stories of the past — either mythical or describing an incident or important event — would be of great interest and value to me.[23]

One should note here that Yovkov talks of using popular myths for purposes of literary creation. Though probably without realizing it, he kept pace with the great artists of this century who discovered the unusual importance of "primitive" sources of creative inspiration for modern art. Unlike his Bulgarian predecessor Petko Todorov, who "used" folkloristic symbols to express his own decadent or Nietzschean vision of the world, Yovkov tries to reveal to the reader the freshness, spontaneity and humaneness of the world view contained in popular myths and legends, and to incorporate it into contemporary culture. In other words, he seeks not to superimpose modern views upon the *Legends*' world outlook, but tries to elicit their own self-contained values: to show "from within" the perspective of what I have called the *naroden* narrator. And in this lie both the originality and the greatness of Yovkov's contribution to Bulgarian literature.

Thematically, *Balkan Legends* may be called a lengthy song in praise of love: both evil, destructive love and good, enabling love. All the "legends" except one — "Koshuta" (The Doe) — share a common denominator: they are love stories with a tragic ending. As for genre, *Balkan Legends* has been defined as "ballads in prose,"[24] a formulation which underlines the collection's strong affinity with oral folklore and romantic tradition in general.

The action of these stories is set before the liberation of Bulgaria, that is, before 1878. Historically, they recreate the atmosphere of life under Turkish rule, which was opposed by two forms of armed resistance: *kurdzhalii* and *khayduti*.[25] In this regard *Balkan Legends* stands apart from all Yovkov's other literary works, which chronologically cover more or less the decade before the outbreak of World War I. *Balkan Legends* also reflects the ethnic diversity of the population of Bulgaria. Their heroes represent all walks of life: poor and wealthy peasants, shepherds, monks, priests, artisans, Turkish officials, robbers, freedom fighters, men and women — all seized by the great passions of love.[26]

One of the most striking examples of this passion is embodied in Shibil, the hero of the story of the same name which opens the volume. Shibil is known for his criminal past, for his violent acts of robbery and murder. He and his men live on human suffering. Turkish officials pursue Shibil to punish him for his cruelty and lawlessness, but it is not their cleverness which puts an end to Shibil's colorful life. One day in the mountains Shibil's robber band meets a group of women. The men expect easy prey, or simply an opportunity to add to their loot. But their hopes are unexpectedly dashed by their leader himself: Shibil catches sight of a girl, Rada, daughter of the local *kekhaya* (senior shepherd) Veliko. He is impressed not only by her beauty but also by her courage: Rada alone does not fear confronting him. He commands that all the women be set free. The encounter with Rada constitutes a turning point in Shibil's life, and in the story. He cannot forget her, and realizes that he must make a crucial decision. In love with Rada, he resolves to quit banditry. The reader does not know for certain whether he expects to be pardoned, but his determination to meet Rada and perhaps marry her is stronger than his fear of death. Rada, moreover, is falsely led to believe by her father that nothing will happen to Shibil if he returns to the village. At the very last moment the *kekhaya* tells the truth: an ambush has been set for Shibil as he enters the village. It is too late to warn him. The dramatic climax is reached when Shibil appears on the street and Rada runs towards him in a desperate attempt to protect him. Both are killed by gunfire.

Further comments on the deeper meaning of "Shibil" should wait upon discussion of another story, such as "Indzhe" (also a proper name), in which is presented a more complicated evolution of the hero. From the exposition of the story we learn that Indzhe is the leader of a large *kurdzhali* band which spreads fear through the ruthless plundering of villages and killings. As Indzhe robs and burns Zheruna, a dialectal name for Zheravna, he meets a girl named Pauna, who becomes his lawful wife and later gives birth to a boy. The hardships of a nomadic life, however, do not foster tenderness or stability. At one point Indzhe becomes so enraged that he grabs the child from Pauna, hits it with a yataghan, throws it to the ground, and leaves it. Soon afterwards Pauna flees Indzhe's camp because she cannot stand living with him any longer. Pauna's disappearance drives Indzhe to the verge of cruel insanity. His rage has no limits, he spares no one and nothing in his way.

There follows an attempt on Indzhe's life when he is wounded by Syaro Barutchiyata, Pauna's relative. As Indzhe recuperates he reflects upon his life, and upon resuming the leadership of his people he is a different man, transformed from bandit chief to popular hero defending the poor. Wherever he goes, he is greeted with joy, flowers and songs. But Indzhe's life ends in tragedy, as do the lives of all the "legendary" heroes. During a visit to Urum-Enikyoy — the village where long ago he abandoned his child — Indzhe receives an enthusiastic welcome. He is happy, friendly and peacefully disposed towards the crowd. Great is his surprise when he spots among the villagers a crippled, humpbacked youth with a rifle. Indzhe is struck by the young man's eyes, which seem familiar to him, but for the moment he wants only to disarm him. At such a friendly gathering Indzhe wants to see no weapons. He asks the youth to hand the rifle over, but the latter refuses. When Indzhe good-humoredly persists, he fires a shot and mortally wounds Indzhe. He dies without realizing that he has been shot by his own son, saved from death after his parents abandoned him in a field not far from the village.

The spiritual evolution of both Shibil and Indzhe is different: Shibil's is simpler and shorter, Indzhe's longer and more complex. Both, however, gradually turn away from evil in order to embrace good. Still, this is only one aspect of their personalities. They are both susceptible to the power of feminine beauty, which in both instances coincides with moral integrity. Shibil is so impressed by Rada's beauty that he is driven to be united with her in life or in death. When Pauna leaves Indzhe, he becomes more cruel than ever, but later on his treasured memories of her and his eagerness to find her again set him on the road to spiritual revival.

Women are equally passionate in their dedication to love, as may be seen in two stories in particular: "Bozhura" (a proper name) and "Prez chuma-voto" (Through the Plague). The former deals with the motif of "sinful love," prominent in earlier stories. Bozhura — the name means 'peony' — is a Gypsy girl who falls in love with Vasilcho, a man of rather dubious moral reputation. Racial and social conditions (Bozhura is a Gypsy and poor, Vasilcho a Bulgarian and rich) do not presage a lasting relationship between the two. Physical attraction, however, is stronger than reason; it cannot be overcome by rational persuasion. When Vasilcho meets Bozhura at a lake, they both give rein to their sensual instincts. Bozhura later has a child, but does not consider this shameful. She proudly bears her "sin." Yovkov's heroes often reveal a typical Shakespearean characteristic: once they initiate a relationship or set an intrigue in motion, they pursue the situation to the very end regardless of the consequences. As long as Vasil-cho lives, Bozhura has a purpose in life. Only when she hears the news of his death does she despair: then she takes her life by drowning.

The daughter of Khadzhi Dragan, Tikha ("Through the Plague"), is also a determined woman, faithful to her emotions, but her determination is even deeper than Bozhura's because of the special circumstances in which it manifests itself. The story has a dramatic setting: the village where Tikha lives is surrounded by plague, and is the last place still untouched by disease. Its people face the ultimate existential situation, as an atmosphere of gloom and doom hangs over the village. The people fear any contact with the outside world may bring the plague to their homes, but they are also threatened by starvation. The only person who can help is Tikha's father, the wealthy Khadzhi Dragan, but he seems unmoved by the situation. In fact, he is busy planning to marry off his daughter to someone she does not particularly like. Her true love, Velichko, has departed, and Tikha does not expect him to return. And then, at the very moment of Tikha's wedding,

Velichko arrives at the church. He is obviously ill with plague, and collapses in front of the altar. People leave the church in panic: the illness has entered the village. Even Velichko's mother does not dare approach him and runs away in horror. The only person who does not abandon him is Tikha, who bends over him and puts his head on her knees. What might have been a happy ending results in tragedy.

Love in Yovkov's world is a lifelong feeling which cannot be eradicated by time. Kraynaliyata, from the story "Na iglikina polyana" (In the Primrose Glade), still remembers his first love although he is now very old and a married man. He sends away his nephew, Stoyan, a *khaydutin* who has taken shelter in his house. Before returning to the woods, Stoyan asks his uncle to lend him his revolver and rifle, thinking Kraynaliyata is too old to need them again. Kraynaliyata, however, follows the old rule of *khaydutin* life: "one does not lend wife, horse or rifle." Instead, he dresses up in his best *khaydutin* clothes and goes off with his nephew. One might expect that Kraynaliyata would rejoin the resistance movement, but instead he tells Stoyan the story of his great love for Kurta, guiding him to the primrose glade where Kurta had been killed by another man — also a *khaydutin* — whom she had rejected in favor of Kraynaliyata. She has remained the most treasured memory of his life. In the end the circle closes: exhausted by his long journey, Kraynaliyata dies in the glade where Kurta was murdered. Stoyan now obtains the revolver and rifle.

To satisfy their desire for love Yovkov's heroes do not hesitate to deceive, to use force, and even to commit sacrilege. Dragota in "Nay-vyarnata strazha" (The Most Faithful Guard) becomes a monk not because of his religious commitment, but because he has no hope of winning his beloved, Ranka. Therefore, when an opportunity arises he does not hesitate to turn the authority of his cassock to his own advantage: he seeks to steal Ranka from the Turkish sultan on the pretext that she should not become the wife of a Muslim. Three men compete for Ranka, each of them using a different method to achieve his goal. Kosan prefers open rebellion; Khadzhi Emin applies force; Dragota resorts to deceit. Yovkov makes it clear that he has no respect for this last tactic. He presents even the sultan, Khadzhi Emin, in a much more positive light than the monk, because his intentions are straightforward.

As in all the other stories of the *Balkan Legends*, so in "The Most Faithful Guard" love leads to tragedy: Kosan is killed and Ranka is abducted to the sultan's residence to become his lawful wife. When after many years she is allowed to visit her native village, she is accompanied by "the most faithful guard" — her two sons.

An individual may enter into various kinds of human relationships, experience different feelings and passions: parental love, religious faith, hatred, the bitterness of disease, the feebleness of old age, but nothing can be stronger or more all-embracing than love for another person. Dochkata, the mother of Velichko in "Through the Plague," deserts her son when she realizes he is diseased, but Tikha remains with him. In spite of his mother's entreaties, Stephen in "The Shepherd's Plaint" will not forgive her for helping those who have thwarted his marriage to Elena. He never returns to his native village, as she wants him to, and descends to an unknown grave. Thus the son punishes his mother for destroying his sacred right to love and find happiness with another person. Old Kraynaliyata stands on the brink of the grave, but he cannot forget Kurta.

In Yovkov's *Legends* love may even justify crime, in the sense that crime may be an unavoidable part of the love relationship. Zhenda ("Postol's Mills") is unfaithful to both her husband and lover, Marin, and must bear the consequences of her behavior: Marin kills both Zhenda and her new lover, a guide for a gypsy caravan. There may be "sinful" love and "ennobling" love, but the narrator draws no moral distinction between the two. He simply suggests that "such is life," whether we like it or not.

Still, all the heroes of the *Legends* remain faithful to themselves. Once they have chosen a course of action, they are consistent in its execution. This is why, probably, one contemporary Bulgarian critic has called *Balkan Legends* "ten hymns to the beauty of human spirituality."[27] Moreover, this spiritual beauty is usually expressed through physical beauty. Yovkov pays a great deal of attention to the physical attractiveness of his characters. In his world, enemies even admire their rivals. When the Turkish effendi sees Shibil coming along the street he exclaims, "What a handsome man!" And when Velichko still insists on firing, he grabs his arm, saying, "Such a man should not die!" Indzhe is handsome too, as are Kosan, Bozhura, Zhenda and even the old Kraynaliyata. Yovkov depicts the world through the prism of his esthetic cult of beauty, a characteristic that runs throughout the whole of his writing like a red thread.

The problem of the genre of *Balkan Legends* also deserves consideration. Yovkov invested much effort in the preparation of this volume, and not merely by gathering folksongs and other material he needed for it. He was also unusually concerned over the final reworking of these stories. As he was still in Bucharest, he asked his best friends in Sofia — the poet Nikolay Liliev and the critic Vladimir Vasilev — to put the final touches to the manuscript before printing.[28] *Balkan Legends* occupies an exceptional place in his literary output. How are we to define the unusual quality of the *Legends*?

I have already mentioned above that in writing *Balkan Legends* Yovkov utilized the riches of Bulgarian folklore. If analyzed in a broader historical and esthetic context, *Balkan Legends* may also be viewed as a literary manifestation of the so-called *Rodno izkustvo* (National Art) movement of the 1920's. After the political catastrophe of World War I and the gradual decline of cosmopolitan Symbolism, the Bulgarian intelligentsia, and artists in particular, sought inspiration in the values of a "national soul," which in turn was associated with the life and popular culture of the peasants.[29] This movement was not provincial, and did not call for parochial isolation. On the contrary, it tried to reveal the "peasant soul" as a combination of both specific national traits and universal values, something which broke down the artificial barriers between national essence and foreign influence, with the latter always being judged as superior to the former. The program of "National Art" found its most evident and interesting expression in the visual arts (the paintings of Ivan Milev) and music (the work of composers Lyubomir Pipkov, Petko Staynov, and Pancho Vladigerov); but literature was not immune to it. And Yovkov's *Balkan Legends* was probably the most significant contribution to this current in the realm of literature. To substantiate this claim one must make a closer examination of Yovkov's use of folklore in these stories.

Yovkov composed the *Legends* in basically two modes. In the first he combines one or two variants of the same folksong (rarely two different songs) with a popular story handed down by tradition or with an insignificant event recorded by history. In the second he combines folksongs alone. It should be pointed out that, regardless of how each "legend" is formed, Yovkov never limits himself to a simple repetition of motifs or their mechanical juxtaposition within a story. Instead he borrows folk motifs creatively; that is, he adapts them to the requirements of his own artistic endeavor. "Shibil," for example, is based on events in the life of a Gypsy, Shibil Mustapha, an historical figure known for his brigandage in the second half of the nineteenth century, and on a popular song commemorating his love for a Bulgarian woman named Dzhenda, a song which apparently has roots in reality too. However, Yovkov handles all these historical data with "poetic license": an ordinary bandit is transformed into a noble figure, and a woman who in reality left her husband and four children is presented as a romantic young girl named Rada.

In similar fashion, the story "Bozhura" is drawn from three different sources. One was a story Yovkov heard as a child about a woman who drowned in a local pond. The other sources are two distinct folksongs: "Vasilcho sedi na kyoshka" (Vasilcho sits on the terrace) and "Nikolcho duma maytsi si..." (Nikolcho tells his mother..."). The first song, which became the compositional core of the entire story, tells of Vasilcho's courtship of Yanka, who is a maid. What separates them is social status. In Yovkov's story the barriers are both social and ethnic: Bozhura is poor and a Gypsy. In the song Vasilcho seems to be serious about his intentions towards Yanka, while in "Bozhura" he is merely flirting, and this defines the tragedy of Bozhura's situation. Thematically, the second song plays a secondary role, merely providing some details of the action.

Yovkov's most interesting use of folklore in prose occurs in "Indzhe." Unlike previous stories, "Indzhe" is based exclusively upon oral poetry. As we have seen above, "Indzhe" reflects an evolution of the hero from robber to defender of the poor. No song registered by folklorists presents Indzhe in just this way. However, there are two principal versions of songs entitled "Indzhe": one shows Indzhe as a ruthless murderer, while the second praises his noble and patriotic deeds. Yovkov's story combines these two versions. Its main thematic core is supplemented by two minor versions of a song about the wounded Indzhe. Finally, there also exists another version of the song which tells of Indzhe's being killed by a small boy. To enliven the action by introducing a love story, Yovkov ties these versions of the song about Indzhe together with one about Kalina, who was, like Pauna, abducted by *kurdzhalii*. Yovkov weaves all these threads together into one artistically consistent entity which belongs not only among Yovkov's finest achievements but also to the treasure house of Bulgarian prose in general.

Whenever critics write of *Balkan Legends*, they emphasize the "lofty" and "heightened" tone of these stories, which are imbued with a high degree of "poeticality." This "poeticality" is achieved through the broad application of stylistic devices borrowed from oral poetry, and, of course, contributes to what I have called the balladic character of the *Legends*. That balladic character is enhanced by yet another important characteristic: the constant presence of supernatural forces in everyday life. In Yovkov the supernatural exists alongside the real, and intervenes effectively in human affairs. The introduction of this element into the *Legends* affects their artistic character less than it does their narrative perspective. That perspective imposes on them a definite philosophical perception of the world, according to which the supernatural is viewed as a genuine part of life. There is no distance between the narrator and his heroes, for he accepts their superstitions and religious beliefs in all seriousness. In "The Doe" — the most pastoral story in the whole collection — Stephen is hunting a doe. Rumor has it that there is something special about the animal, that it possesses the eyes of a human being. Stephen is warned not to kill it, and yet he persists in the hunt.

When finally he spots the doe and "aims his rifle at her heart," there suddenly appears beside the doe a woman milking it. And this recurs each time the hunter aims at the animal. In "Postol's Mills" the story opens with a description of the arrival of a black billy-goat at Vurban's mill. Popular belief holds goats to be creatures of the devil, and a black billy-goat always foreshadows bad luck. In "Indzhe" an old priest curses Indzhe shortly before he is wounded. One could cite other examples illustrating the invisible power of supernatural forces.

To be sure, this particular characteristic of the *Legends* does not in itself define their balladic nature; it merely contributes to it, in combination with other artistic qualities. As a genre, the ballad contains three structural elements: those of epic, lyric and drama.[30] All three are present in the *Legends*. Their strongest underlying component is, no doubt, the epic. As for the other two components, their importance varies from one story to another. Yovkov evokes lyricism either by stressing the role of nature or by extensive use of inversion, which means a departure from the normative and commonly accepted Bulgarian word order. He achieves dramatic effect, on the other hand, by presenting his hero as the embodiment of a discord between the life of ordinary persons and his own life as "outsider" in the moral but not the social sense of the word. Through their behavior Shibil, Kraynaliyata, Indzhe, Bozhura, Zhenda express disapproval of their own moral credo; they revolt against their hitherto established way of life. Hence it can be said that the dramatic character of these stories is implicit in the psychological predispositions of their characters.

Thus, like any great writer, Yovkov penetrates to the depths of human feelings and passions. He does this not by lengthy psychological analysis, but by careful and sparing description of their behavior and reactions to other people. And this modern creative approach places Yovkov within the ranks of the most interesting writers of this century. While writing seemingly historical stories, Yovkov examines the eternal problems of human existence. However, the historical framework of the *Legends* should not be dismissed as mere "decoration" only. It also tells us much about the national destiny of a country which for almost five hundred years remained under Turkish domination and yet managed to preserve its identity. "Indzhe" is not merely a story about its hero's personal tragedy; it also depicts the growing strength and maturity of the *khayduti* movement as a conscious force of resistance against the Turks. "Yunashki glavi" (The Heads of Heroes) describes a tragic episode from the April uprising of 1876 against the Turks; "The Most Faithful Guard" is not only a story about the unfulfilled love of Kosan and Ranka, but also an illustration of Turkish coercion: Khadzhi Emin uses his power as a Turkish ruler to abduct Ranka and force her to become his wife. Throughout the centuries thousands of Bulgarian women had shared Ranka's destiny by becoming wives or mistresses of Turkish officials.

It is precisely Yovkov's skill at melding historical atmosphere with universal motifs that makes *Balkan Legends* a national epic of international stature.

IV   EVENINGS AT THE ANTIMOVO INN

Almost concurrently with *Legends* Yovkov wrote[31] his *Vecheri v Antimovskiya khan* (Evenings at the Antimovo Inn), which appeared in 1928, one year after *Balkan Legends*. The volume contained seven stories in a cycle centered about the inn at Antimovo, and nine additional stories on a variety of themes, of which the most important are "Po zhitsata" (Along the Wire) and "Albena." *Evenings at the Antimovo Inn* is in effect a hymn in praise of Dobrudzha, an idealization of its life as Yovkov had known it between 1900, when he began to teach there, and the outbreak of the Great War in 1914. There was no real village of Antimovo, much less any inn there. The inn is a fictional and symbolic place of action created in the writer's imagination, a setting for stories which reproduce the atmosphere of the "good old times." When asked by Dimo Minev about the location of the Antimovo inn, a teacher from Dobrudzha answered: "In the whole of Dobrudzha." In the opening sentence of the very first story, "Dryamkata na Kalmuka" (Kalmuk's Nap), the narrator says that the Antimovo inn is not simply located at a crossroad, but at a place where *many* [italics mine] roads intersect. According to Simeon Sultanov,[32] this sentence introduces the central theme of the entire cycle, which is the flow of life itself, its constant transitoriness on the one hand and its constancy on the other. People arrive as visitors from various directions and depart in different directions. Some of them come to relax in the cozy atmosphere of the inn, some are attracted by the charm of the innkeeper, Sarandovitsa, and the beauty of her daughter, young Sarandovitsa.

Moreover, the ever-flowing "river of life" manifests itself not only in the constant coming and going of guests, but also by events which occur in and around the Antimovo inn. Driven by jealousy, the teacher in "Kalmuk's Nap" makes an attempt on young Sarandovitsa's life: he cannot accept the fact that she plans to marry the young and handsome Zakharko. In an unusual adventure, Palazov in "Chastniyat uchitel" (The Tutor) falls in love with Miss Schmidt, a circus performer, and leaves Antimovo with her. Khristo Mesechkata in "Vragove" (Enemies) plays upon a continuing hostility between the two villages of Surneno and Bistra. When some peasants from Bistra stop at the inn, Mesechkata regales them with jokes about the alleged stupidity of their enemies. However, as soon as they leave the inn and a party from the other village arrives, he makes exactly the same sort of comments about the inhabitants of Bistra. In each case Mesechkata is rewarded with drink and good food.

The inn witnesses human tragedy and joy, laughter and tears, deceit and honesty. The festivity of the ordinary permeates the mood of the inn, exactly as in life. And over this vivid and variegated flow of life reigns the towering figure of young Sarandovitsa, who becomes the innkeeper after her mother's death. Her shrewd, even cunning manner of dealing with customers is at times balanced by sheer generosity and human warmth. She displays remarkable sobriety in running her business, and this characteristic, combined with her physical attractiveness, brings an eager clientele to the inn.

And so life goes on. The Antimovo inn houses guests. Sarandovitsa stands behind the counter, welcoming them, as her bodyguard Kalmuk dozes in a corner of the dining room and keeps an eye on potential troublemakers. Despite the mutability of outside events, the inn itself embodies the idea of stability through the continuing ownership of it by three generations of Sarandovitsas (grandmother, mother and daughter), and through the everlasting presence of Kalmuk, who has been there as long as anyone can remember. It is clear that Yovkov admires the established order of things, loves tradition and the people of the past.

Although in *Evenings at the Antimovo Inn* Yovkov describes everyday life, in fact he presents unusual characters who, despite some weaknesses, are distinguished for their simplicity, sincerity, and readiness to enter into genuine human relationships. Yovkov's attitude toward these aspects of human nature is most prominently expressed in the two final stories of the cycle: "Sreshta" (Encounter) and "Shepa pepel" (Handful of Ashes). In the former, Vitan Chaush, a retired police officer, visits the inn for the first time in twenty years. He is now an old man blind in one eye, which he lost while pursuing a bandit, Solakolu Redzheb. Vitan Chaush's return to the inn brings back memories of the past, and he tells the story of how he lost his eye. In conclusion, however, he does not regret his misfortune, and feels no anger at Redzheb's mother, who made him half-blind. What really upsets him is the harsh truth that the good times of his youth are forever gone. At one point in the story Chaush turns to a musician and says: "Play something for us. But I do not want new songs. Play an old, melancholy, heroic song."[33] And he repeats that request at the end of the tale.

The cycle's closing story, "Handful of Ashes," stresses its central theme in more than one way. Notwithstanding Yovkov's sympathy for patriarchal society, his attachment to it and his desire to preserve its forms and traditional values, the main underlying theme of this cycle is the idea of transitoriness, of the ebb and flow of life. Nothing endures forever. This rule has no exceptions, and the Antimovo inn as a symbol of the "good old times" is as fully subject to it as anything else. Invaders come and destroy everything: the inn goes up in flames, Sarandovitsa and Kalmuk are killed. All that remains is a handful of ashes and memories. And on this note Yovkov ends the cycle. He does not go beyond this point of destruction, because whatever happened later does not excite his imagination. The ending of *Evenings at the Antimovo Inn* is almost symbolic for the whole of Yovkov's writing.

A few words ought to be said about other stories included in this volume, especially "Along the Wire" and "Albena." As in many other works, the plot of "Along the Wire" is based on a superstition about a "white swallow" which brings luck and heals people.[34] The hero of the story is a poor peasant in search of such a white swallow. Three of his children have died of a mysterious disease, and the origin of his last daughter's illness is also explained supernaturally.[35] The father decides to put his sick daughter in a cart and set out along the roads that follow the telephone wires, hoping the girl will catch a glimpse of a white swallow sitting on a wire and thus be saved from death. The most touching aspect of this narrative is the peasant's genuine belief in the power of this formula for healing, and in the simplicity of his description of the misfortune that has struck his family. Furthermore, it expresses the writer's own resolute conviction that, although art should describe human worries, sufferings and tragedy, it also has an obligation to bring a message of hope and consolation.

In other stories — for example "Imane" (Money) and "Senebirskite bratya" (Brothers from Senebir) — Yovkov depicts the dehumanizing effect of money and the destructive impact of greed on the human personality. In "Drugoselets" (A Peasant from Another Village) he expresses great compassion for the sufferings of a humble man who has lost the most faithful helper a peasant can have — his horse.

Moral issues remain constantly at the center of Yovkov's attention, but not all of them are resolved in accordance with the patriarchal code of ethics. One of the most memorable stories of this volume is "Albena."

Albena, a beautiful woman accused of murdering her husband, is being taken to jail by two policemen. There is evidence that she was assisted in this crime by her lover, but nobody knows who the man is and Albena refuses to name him. Her fellow villagers are filled with indignation. However, when Albena appears in the street, led by two policemen, the crowd is awed by her beauty. Suddenly one of the peasants cannot imagine their village without Albena, and he shouts: "Boys, let's keep her, don't give her away. What is our village without Albena!" If in other stories the motif of "sinful" beauty or "sinful" love occurs as a thematic break, in "Albena" it finds its full-fledged realization, as Yovkov's cult of beauty reaches its peak. Two years after the appearance of *Evenings at the Antimovo Inn* Yovkov decided to recast "Albena" as a play.

His three volumes of stories published in the 1920's established Yovkov as a leading Bulgarian writer. In 1929, on the recommendation of the Bulgarian Academy of Sciences, Yovkov received the Kiril and Metodi prize for literature. And he himself felt that it was the time to experiment in a different literary genre. He opted for the drama.

CHAPTER 4

Yovkov's Dramaturgy

It is characteristic that in his book on Yovkov, Simeon Sultanov entitles the chapter on drama "Unpleasantness."[1] Indeed, the critics reacted negatively to his first drama, *Albena*, when it was staged in the spring of 1929, and unfortunately, his three further plays — *Milionerut* (The Millionaire, 1930), *Boryana* (1932), and *Obiknoven chovek* (An Ordinary Person, 1936) — suffered the same fate. The last play, as a matter of fact, came entirely to grief; and even if the writer had lived longer, he would probably have never returned to this genre.

Yovkov developed an interest in drama very early. As a student in the First Sofia Gymnasium (upper school), he participated in school plays staged by his fellow pupils. Later on, in Dobrudzha, he organized an amateur theater and served as director, stage designer and actor. Drama was his "second love." After his failure in poetry and his achievement of recognition in prose, he decided to try his hand at the dramatic genre.

No doubt Yovkov was aware of the dangers associated with this new adventure. First of all, there existed very little in the way of a national theatrical tradition. The sentimental drama *Ivanko* (1872) by Vasil Drumev (1841–1901), a few historical dramas by Ivan Vazov, Modernist and Symbolist plays by Petko Todorov and Peyo Yavorov constituted Yovkov's principal inheritance from the native past. Neither could he count on a tradition of acting. Bulgarian theater was still in its swaddling-clothes and the quality of acting left much to be desired, to say the least. Among the Russian emigres who settled in Bulgaria after the revolution of 1917 was Nikolay Osipovich Masalitinov (1880–1961), a former member of the Moscow Art Theater, and a pupil of Konstantin Stanislavsky. He arrived in Sofia in 1925 and became the leading director of the Bulgarian National Theater. However, Masalitinov was staunchly devoted to realistic theater and thwarted attempts to develop other theatrical techniques. Later, in his conversations with Kazandzhiev, Yovkov criticized Masalitinov, saying his "too realistic" method deprived the theater of "poetic atmosphere."[2] Yovkov blamed him partially for the failure of his plays.

Despite these unfavorable circumstances, Yovkov decided to take the risks of becoming a playwright and exposing himself to a broader audience. It was therefore natural that in turning to drama he should at the same time return to a favorite theme: the role of beauty — or, more precisely, the role of feminine beauty — in human destiny. Out of his four plays, two were devoted to women: *Albena* and *Boryana*. Until now Bulgarian criticism has treated these two plays separately, but I believe they should be discussed jointly as two aspects or two poles of one question. I shall therefore disregard chronology in order to analyze *Boryana* before *The Millionaire*.

I *ALBENA*

Albena is an adaptation of the short story of the same title. However, in transposing prose to drama, Yovkov could not avoid introducing significant changes in the presentation of characters and the content itself. While the core of the plot remains the same — Albena, a beautiful married woman, is in love with Nyagul, a married man; Albena's husband Kutsar is murdered, and the lovers are suspected of committing the crime — the details of its realization are different. In the drama Albena often visits the mill to see Nyagul, who works there. Her beauty attracts the attention of many visitors coming to the village to grind corn. Among them is a young, wealthy and handsome man, Ivan Senebirski, who makes approaches to Albena and insistently offers her work at his farm. In the story Senebirski is mentioned in passing only as a "handsome, fair-haired man" who asks about Albena; in the play his role is expanded considerably. He is the only person who discovers the true nature of the relationship between Albena and Nyagul. After his unsuccessful wooing of Albena, he tells Kutsar that his wife is Nyagul's mistress, and sets in motion the chain of events which leads to a tragic resolution, the murder. Nyagul's role is also considerably broadened in the drama. In the short story, he appears at the end only to admit his guilt. In the play he is a rather vicious character, the driving force behind the crime and its sole perpetrator.

And what of Albena? Her common characteristic in both the story and the play is her unusual beauty. Her charm is irresistible. Both old and young fall under the spell of her beauty, and women envy her physical appearance. But while in the story Albena is an accomplice to the crime (she helps Nyagul strangle her husband), in the play she is not. In the story she remains cool, detached, almost cruel: after all, she committed the crime in cold blood. "This woman was sinful," says the narrator, "but beautiful." In order to underline the "sinful" nature of her beauty, Yovkov has Albena don her best attire before being led away for questioning to the office of the village administrator. This episode is played down in the drama; but it is exactly at this point that Albena admits[3] she puts on these clothes in order to emphasize the facet of her personality which brought her to ruin. Consequently, the Albena of the play is more humble, apologetic about her behavior, and remorseful even though she has not committed the crime. As a matter of fact, she tries to dissuade Nyagul from killing Kutsar. As the drama ends, the people are ready to forgive Albena her sin, though not in the story.

According to Sultanov, this transformation occurs because of Yovkov's desire to "save" Albena from condemnation as a demoralizing force, to "save" beauty from being judged as a factor contributing to immorality.[4] Sultanov's book is the best written to date on Yovkov, but one is inclined to take issue with his suggestion that Yovkov wanted to preserve what he calls "the ascendant power of beauty." How is this "ascendant power" of beauty supposed to influence things? For the better, of course. Now if such was indeed Yovkov's intention, then he failed to carry it out, because, voluntarily or involuntarily, Albena destroys Nyagul's marriage and her own, thus acting as an agent of evil. Albena's intentions may be good, but that which happens within the text itself is not.

As a play *Albena* suffers from a lack of *dramatic focus*. The author wants to show the spectator too many things. A first reading of the text may leave the impression that it describes a typical "love triangle." In fact, the play also deals with the question of a woman's right to control her own lot: Albena is liberated because she dares to love a married man, and so follows her own impulses. In addition, there are elements of social drama as well. Yovkov introduces a new figure in the play, Andrey, who expresses indignation at Albena's behavior and speaks for traditional moral values. He condemns Albena unequivocally, demanding lynch-mob retribution for her "sinful" love. Finally, there is the question of the role of beauty in people's lives, which has already been mentioned. Yovkov probably wished to emphasize this latter aspect of the play, although not in the sense suggested by Sultanov. In the drama Yovkov was probably intentionally ambiguous about Albena's character, and this was perhaps why he complained of Masalitinov's excessive realism in staging his plays.

Yovkov admitted that he had constructed the image of Albena in the play on a different "ethical basis"[5] than the one in the short story. In the story Albena is unidimensional; she shows no regret over killing Kutsar and can be easily interpreted, while the second Albena is more complex, deeper and thus multidimensional, although the factor determining her destiny remains the curse of her "sinful" beauty." Consequently, Albena's situation may be interpreted also as a kind of personal drama, because her subjective intentions do not coincide with the objective course of events, and in the end she unleashes forces of evil in human beings. I might even say that Albena is Yovkov's first character to be fully aware of this tragic conflict. In Yovkov's view, beauty — and feminine beauty in particular — is not always linked with ethical integrity; it does not necessarily engender noble deeds, although Yovkov seems to favor this correlation. Albena tends to represent the destructive power of beauty. In this regard she is contrasted with Boryana, the subject of Yovkov's second play about woman. While Albena represents the negative pole of beauty and love, Boryana constitutes the positive, because her beauty attracts goodness. In this context, then, both plays become more understandable. In creating them Yovkov, I believe, wanted to present the two symbolic halves of the truth about beauty and its impact on men.

II *BORYANA*

Boryana may be called a dramatized story about a peasant family made up of a father (Zlatil), three sons (Rali, Andrey, Pavli), and two daughters-in-law (Vida, the wife of Rali, and Elitsa, the wife of Andrey). They live together in one house in accordance with the patriarchal tradition of family relationships. However, the first act shows that all is not well: the family is torn apart by enmity between individual brothers, on the one hand, and the children and the father, on the other. The brothers accuse one another of not working hard enough to maintain the well-being of the household, while the father remains under the suspicion of hiding a large amount of money which he supposedly had stolen long ago from his own father, thus partially contributing to his death. The villain of the family, the most ruthlessly malicious character in the play, is Rali, the eldest son, who clearly represents the forces of evil. He and his wife Vida search every corner of the house and yard looking for his father's hidden treasure. He accuses Andrey of being a drunkard and a tramp; he also wants to thwart Pavli's marriage because this would increase the number of family members to share in Zlatil's money. Rali's ideal solution would be to get rid of his two brothers, then find the money and keep it for himself. His greed makes him dangerous and a threat to all family ties. Zlatil is also obsessed with his money, and guards it from the watchful eyes of his sons (especially Rali) by constantly changing its hiding place.

Into this poisonous atmosphere of suspicion and hatred enters Boryana, Pavli's fiancee, who has left her own home because her father would not allow her to marry Pavli. Boryana comes from a rich family, and Pavli is no match for her. This illicit situation gives Rali a pretext for protesting against her presence in the house and demanding she be sent back home to the village of Alfatavi. Not all, however, share Rali's objections to her. To be sure, she has violated the rules of patriarchal order by moving into Pavli's family home before getting married: she is liberated in her love, and in this sense resembles some of Yovkov's other heroines, including Albena. But this is not Boryana's most important characteristic. Her beauty is coupled with goodness: as Andrey says of her, "She is worth more than money, more than treasure." He feels that he may have gained an important ally in her. Andrey and his wife Elitsa are at odds with Rali, but his influence is insignificant because he is only the second son. He is tired of quarrels, hatred, and his father's stinginess; consequently he does not enjoy staying home, and seeks respite in helping other people, in defending the poor, rather like Grozdan from *The Harvester*. He is the only one who understands the importance of Boryana's presence for the family's well-being. When he hears her singing, he calls her "a swallow." Boryana offers love to everyone in the house, including those unfriendly to her. The very moment Boryana enters Zlatil's house, the play shifts from a drama of characters to a drama of ethical values, a drama of ideas. The conflict rages between money — the symbol of evil that divides the family — and the motif of the singing bird, the symbol of goodness personified by Boryana.

Money as a destructive force in human relationships had been treated earlier by Elin Pelin in his powerful novelette *Geratsite* (The Gerak Family). The two works share some external similarities of plot. The Gerak family is also composed of three sons and an old father who is stingy, hides his money, and fears his children's plotting against him. The family is torn apart by hostility and destroyed. The literary newspaper *Literaturen glas* (Literary Voice) at the time came close to accusing Yovkov of plagiarism.[6] Yovkov replied in a short explanatory note published in the paper *Zora*[7] (Dawn). He indicated that he drew the idea of *Boryana* from his own story "Imane" (Treasure, 1927), which was included in *Evenings at the Antimovo Inn*. But *Boryana* can hardly be called an adaptation of "Treasure." The story tells of a dying old woman who hides her money from her two daughters and sons-in-law. For years this money has hung over the family like a curse which prevented children and parents from establishing close and loving relationships. The old woman decides not to reveal where the money is hidden, and dies taking her secret with her. According to Yovkov, *Boryana* had yet another source: reality itself. In the same note, he explained that his friend Petko Tishelov, a teacher from Kharmanli, had

told him of an old peasant who kept his money hidden from his sons. After
one of them found and stole it, the father died of despair. "Even in its raw
state," commented Yovkov, "this event contains, as one can see, all the data
to be found in my play."[8] Later Tishelov confirmed that in conversations
with him Yovkov had shown a special interest in such themes as "stinginess," "hidden money," "wealth," and "family quarrels."[9] Tishelov rightly
noted that creative sources of the same kind can be found in other works of
world literature by such writers as Plautus, Molière, and Nikolay Gogol.

But even without Yovkov's explanation, one can easily discern the
difference between his play and *The Gerak Family*. Elin Pelin was very consistent in showing the destructive power of money, and took the story to
the bitter end, as the Geraks as a family are destroyed and the patriarchal
order disintegrates. Yovkov, the great moralist, wants to preserve as much
of the old order as possible. This in turn determines Boryana's role. She
brings to the house of Zlatil the love, trust and joy it needs so much. Her
goodness is contagious, and gradually, she wins the hearts of everyone in
the family. She dares to speak openly with Zlatil about his money; and
when she accidentally finds out where it is hidden, she tells him. She thus
gains Zlatil's trust, and begins his transformation. He realizes that Boryana
does not wish to destroy him but to save him. At the end of the play he
admits:

> This money! I hid it for thirty years ... I listened to the devil. I served the
> devil. It's good that Boryana came ... As if God has brought her. Finished. I
> feel relieved.[10]

And he decides to divide his money equally among his sons. The "singing
bird" achieves its goal of bringing reconciliation and harmony to the whole
family. Earlier Yovkov had exploited the motif of the bird as messenger of
hope in "Along the Wire." Now he considerably expands its function in a
new direction: it acts as the powerful herald of moral good. In other words,
Yovkov elevates the moral to the category of the esthetic, in what one critic
has called "esthetization of the good."[11]

As a dramatist, however, Yovkov paid a high price for his moralizing
tendencies. Contrary to the laws of dramatic structure, *Boryana* concludes
with a happy ending, which, in my judgment, blunts the initial sharpness of
the play's central conflict. Boryana also manages to settle the conflict with
her own father, and receives his permission to marry Pavli. Consequently,
at the end she emerges not only as the savior of Zlatil's family, and the
defender of patriarchal order, but also as an independent, liberated woman.
In *Boryana* Yovkov may have succeeded in creating an alternative to

Albena, but he once again failed as a dramatist. *Boryana* reminds us more of a pastoral than a drama.

III   *THE MILLIONAIRE*

The theme of money recurs in Yovkov's only comedy, *The Millionaire*, which, surprisingly bears witness to Yovkov's superb understanding of the secrets of the genre. I say "surprisingly" because one might have expected that he would have felt less at ease with comedy, for Yovkov's prose contains more dramatic elements than comic. In fact Yovkov was never a "dry" prose writer, but humor was hardly one of his strengths. One may also speculate as to whether the relatively favorable public reception of *The Millionaire* had anything to do with Yovkov's later decision to experiment with satirical prose by creating *Priklyucheniya na Gorolomov* (Gorolomov's Adventures).

The plot of *The Millionaire* has a typical comic twist: a character believed to be quite wealthy proves to be destitute. The intrigue develops as Mr. Maslarski, a respectable citizen in a small provincial town in Dobrudzha tries to organize a new musical society for the purpose of stimulating an appreciation for music among inhabitants of the town. According to the founding members of the society, music not only ennobles people, it also brings them closer together. At one meeting various distinguished individuals from the local community are nominated as members of the society. However, when the name of the veterinarian Khristo Kondov is mentioned, Mr. Maslarski and some others object. They dislike him for being permissive, odd, and for violating the rules of patriarchal order. Mr. Maslarski even claims that Kondov's indecent behavior has caused him to send his daughter Evgeniya out of town. This situation changes abruptly in the course of the meeting, however, when someone declares that Kondov has become a millionaire. The news has a magic effect. Now everyone agrees that Kondov would be a desirable member, and Mr. Maslarski does not limit himself to proposing his acceptance: he even nominates him for honorary president. While he is at it, Mr. Maslarski also changes his story as to why his daughter chose to live on the family estate outside town: she wished, it now seems, to enjoy the fresh country air.

As news of Kondov's supposed wealth spreads, he becomes the target of much attention from the ladies. At the same time, he makes no attempt to inform his fellow citizens that the money which has been received in the bank is not his, but belongs to another person of the same name. Consequently, one of his admirers, Khristina, even attempts to arrange a phony engagement with him: while he is asleep in a tavern, she takes off his ring and replaces it with her own. The next day Kondov learns, much to his surprise, that he is engaged. But the most energetic attempts to "conquer" Kondov are made by Mrs. Maslarski. On the pretext that Kondov needs peace and comfort for his work (but in reality with her daughter in mind), Mrs. Maslarski proposes to rent the doctor a room in her house, then almost forcibly takes him there and locks him up along with her husband. While she is off to bring her daughter Evgeniya back to town, Mr. Maslarski is supposed to entertain Kondov by playing cards. When the latter gets bored and wants to leave, he realizes that the door is locked and he is virtually a prisoner of the Maslarskis.

In the meantime, Mrs. Maslarski does not realize that Evgeniya and Kondov are already in love, and so it will be a simple matter to arrange a marriage between them. As soon as Evgeniya has returned, Mrs. Maslarski leaves her alone with Kondov, and then comes back after a short time to find the couple embracing and kissing each other. After expressing her "indignation," Mrs. Maslarski declares that, having besmirched the reputation of the family, Kondov has no choice but to marry Evgeniya. Both hastily agree to this demand, but they also decide to conceal the truth about Kondov's fortune. If before they were "victims" of a plot, now they turn into plotters themselves. The marriage takes place immediately and the happy couple leave for their honeymoon. At the end, the Maslarskis received a letter from Kondov in which he tells them that he is not a millionaire and explains why he had kept his true financial status secret. Mrs. Maslarski comes close to a breakdown, and vows to undo the marriage.

The Millionaire consists of four acts. In the first we learn of Maslarski's intention to organize the musical society, and of the fact that Kondov is supposedly a millionaire. The second act shows the impact of the news about Kondov on local people, especially women. The third is entirely devoted to Mrs. Maslarski's efforts to arrange a marriage between her daughter and Kondov, while the fourth gradually reveals the truth about Kondov's financial condition.

In spite of some weaknesses (for example, the secondary characters remain indistinct), *The Millionaire* is an entertaining "comedy of errors," and has remained popular with the public to this day. The critics, however, are of another mind. In his discussion of Yovkov's plays, for instance, Sultanov does not mention *The Millionaire* at all. Others have rebuked Yovkov for excessive dependance on Gogol's *Revizor*[12] (The Inspector-General), the last act in particular provides some justification for such accusations. It recalls the penultimate scene in *The Inspector-General*, when the postmaster reads a letter revealing the fact that "the inspector was not an inspector." In the final scene of *The Millionaire* Maslarski reads Kondov's letter, which makes it clear that the "millionaire was not a millionaire" at all. Such accusations, however, have to do with the formal aspects of the play, and not its content. It is much more surprising that Marxist critics have never tried to highlight the play's elements of social criticism.[13] And such elements do exist, both in the plot and in the presentation of characters. The driving force behind the action of *The Millionaire* is money, and Yovkov shows its corrupting power. It engenders greed, fosters hypocrisy, and as a consequence destroys human relationships. In fact, no one except Evgeniya is immune to the disease of money-madness. Although she knows Kondov is not a millionaire, she still wants to marry him, and deserves credit for that. Every other character is affected by the news of Kondov's money in a negative way. Indeed, Yovkov's play is a harsh condemnation of a society based on material values, but somehow this aspect has remained unnoticed.

In general, Yovkov's plays were given a progressively more unfavorable critical recognition. While *Albena* was praised — albeit with some reservations — as an interesting play, later on some critics asked whether *Boryana* could be called a drama[14] at all; and they considered *The Millionaire* an insignificant comedy. But the worst fate befell *An Ordinary Person*: Masalitinov commented that it simply passed "unnoticed."[15] It was, as Sultanov puts it, "a sad epilogue" to Yovkov's efforts as a playwright.

IV   *AN ORDINARY PERSON*

In *An Ordinary Person* Yovkov attempted to create a social drama. It is also the only work in which he dealt with the urban theme, one which is, as Moser has rightly observed, "noticeably absent from his novels and short stories."[16] Thus he responded to the critics' demands that he abandon the description of rural, patriarchal mores to describe the reality of the modern city. It is also a drama with a clear-cut thesis: it seeks to respond to the problem of good and evil in life.

Anichka, a young girl with noble dreams and an optimistic approach to life, meets Aleksander Strumski, who seems to share her perception of the world, and, inexperienced as she is, soon decides to share her life with him. Very soon, however, her illusions are destroyed: Strumski proves to be a criminal and a swindler. He is arrested and dies in a hospital. Anichka is left alone with a child, the fruit of her unhappy affair with Strumski.

Anichka is in deep despair, and thinks of committing suicide but the child keeps a spark of hope alive within her. At this point she meets Boris Brankov, a man by no means a stranger to her: she had met him in the past as a young girl, but rejected his love, for he was a broker, and seemed too dull and "ordinary" to be seriously considered as a husband. Now, when Anichka is almost destitute, he is the one who lends her a helping hand.

Though others, for example, Rashko and his wife Stamenka, may sympathize with Anichka, Brankov is the only one both willing and able to help. He is a man of stable convictions, and his love for Anichka has endured, but his social status has changed. After much travel abroad, Brankov has gained considerable financial experience and become a successful businessman. He resolved to build a factory to create jobs for the poor and jobless. At the end of the play Yovkov depicts something resembling a pastoral oasis of happiness. Sokolovets, the place where the factory is built, becomes an earthly paradise where workers live in comfortable apartments, stroll in beautiful parks and enjoy recreational facilities. They glorify Brankov, an "ordinary person" who has become a hero: he is not only Anichka's moral savior, but also a social reformer.

It is beside the point to ask whether a story like this is realistic or purely imaginary. Surely such events could have taken place. A much more relevant question is the extent to which such a plot could serve as material for the dramatic genre. The answer is closely tied to Yovkov's outlook on life. No doubt the author of *An Ordinary Person* wanted to warn his audience against "strong," "interesting," "inspiring" and "rebellious" individuals of the Strumski type, whom he considered destructive. However, by introducing Brankov as his chief hero, he removed the source of conflict as a leading dramatic device. Yovkov makes Brankov succeed because society wants him to succeed: there is a tacit agreement on that on both sides. More than that, Yovkov transfers his patriarchal, idealistic solutions from traditional rural society and injects them into a different social milieu, ignoring the obvious discrepancy between idealistically patriarchal ideas and the harsh realities of modern city life. To be more precise: Yovkov presents himself as a poet of social concord who rejects social conflict as destructive. This idea had emerged for the first time in his novelette *The Harvester*, and recurred in *Chiflikut kray granitsata* (The Farm at the Frontier, 1934). The theme outlined in the earlier novels becomes almost a symbol in *An Ordinary Person*.

In short, while the moral idea of the dramatic plot in *An Ordinary Person* has some merit and embodies the writer's noble intentions, it is highly unsuitable as thematic material for dramatic realization. Consequently, *An*

Ordinary Person was doomed to failure from the very moment of its inception. After only one theatrical season (1935–1936) it vanished from the National Theater, never to reappear again on any Bulgarian stage. Certainly the political regime established after 1944 did not look favorably upon it.

Despite their lack of success with the public, Yovkov's dramas cannot be entirely dismissed as insignificant. Although technically defective, they contain certain possibilities, and within the framework of the Bulgarian national theater they constitute an important episode in its history. Yovkov brought to Bulgarian theater an ethical dimension which it needed badly, for it had long been dominated by historical, national and social themes. Though unsuccessful in diverting its course, he showed it the right direction, and his search for new artistic and thematic paths deserves respect. Yovkov's lack of success in the theater was mainly due to his misunderstanding of drama as a specific genre. He insisted that drama "is also epic,"[17] and this error of judgment affected all his plays, for in them the epic component definitely outweighs the dramatic. But Yovkov may have been right in blaming directors for staging his plays inappropriately. Both *Albena* and *Boryana* were — and to my knowledge still are — played as realistic dramas of everyday life (*bitovi drami*). Such an interpretation deprives them of their depth. They are more suitable for a metaphoric type of theater, which stresses not realistic details of action or characterization, but the significance of ideas. Both *Albena* and *Boryana* are hyperboles, or symbols of moral ideas, and they should be staged as such. If in the future these dramas find imaginative stage directors, they may eventually emerge as more significant works than they have until now.

CHAPTER 5

Continuation and Change: The Prose of the Thirties

Despite his failures with his first dramas, Yovkov entered the 1930's with confidence and an amazingly intense creative drive. He was by then a celebrity, a recognized and established national writer. His financial situation seemed secure too: he could buy a modest apartment near the beautiful city park, and could ensure the material welfare of his wife and daughter. Although never prone to socialize with other writers or people in general, he had a small circle of friends whom he met quite regularly in various Sofia coffeehouses. A frequent coffeehouse companion was Spiridon Kazandzhiev, a psychology professor at the University of Sofia and the author of *Meetings and Conversations with Yordan Yovkov*. Kazandzhiev gathered most of the material for his book during his encounters with the writer in coffeehouses. Yovkov told him how much he enjoyed visiting them, and even called one of them his "second home."[1] He explained that actually he "wrote" most of his stories at coffee tables, and then "rewrote" them at home before publishing them. Yovkov's habit of "working" in coffeehouses was well known to some of his friends: Kazandzhiev recalled that he avoided joining Yovkov in the coffeehouses between 5 and 7 in the evening because he knew the writer was "at work" then and did not want to disturb him.

Indeed Yovkov's ability to concentrate on his work was admirable. As Sultanov has noted, Yovkov took no holidays: he knew weekdays only. Indeed in the last seven years of his life he produced two novels, two collections of short stories, and three plays, slightly more than half of his total literary output.

But there were reasons for concern too. Critics and friends complained of a certain monotony in his prose, his constantly looking backward at the past at the expense of the present, and so on. Probably Yovkov himself felt that some of these criticisms were justified. His turn to drama in the early 1930's may have been a response to such reservations, and his own fears of becoming one-sided. Consequently, he sought to broaden the whole gamut of his literary experience, both in content and form. Aside from his foray into the theater, he dreamed his whole life of writing a novel. Perhaps this explains his preference for broad, epic narrative cycles rather than short stories with single motifs or themes. The prime example of this is, of course, the collection *Evenings at the Antimovo Inn*, with its common protagonists and a structure reminiscent of a novel. But even *Balkan Legends* may be regarded as a sort of cycle, for it is set in one region and devoted to essentially one theme: love. Some other characteristics of his short prose point toward the novel: for example, the recurrence of the same setting in various works; one can quote Filip's Inn in "Serafim," *The Farm at the Frontier*, "Nespoluka" (Misfortune) and other stories. The motif of disputes over land appears in "The Trial," *Evenings at the Antimovo Inn, The Harvester,* and *The Farm at the Frontier*. "Yes," writes Sultanov, "we have the feeling that we are reading chapters from one and the same book which, unfortunately, remained unfinished."[2]

Yovkov had no experience in writing novels. He called his first longer prose work, *The Harvester* (1920), a novella. This means that he began to write his first "true" novel approximately ten years later, twenty years after his prose debut, concurrently with his plays (*The Millionaire; Boryana*) and also with a second novel, *Gorolomov's Adventures. The Farm at the Frontier* appeared serially in the pages of the journal *Zora* (Dawn) in 1933–34, and as a separate book in 1934.

I   THE FARM AT THE FRONTIER

The Farm at the Frontier contains an important innovation: for the first time in his prose,[3] Yovkov places the historical time of the action in the postwar period, after 1918. He therefore went beyond the usual limits of his interest in the patriarchal past and strove for contemporaneity. This temporal shift has a direct impact on the nature of the novel: it describes the gradual decay of a huge rural estate (*chiflik*), which is a remnant of the old, traditional order. The farm belongs to Manolaki, who is said to have acquired large pieces of land in the past by shady dealings. His fraud has been discovered, and the government has taken a considerable part of his land away for distribution to the peasants. Later, as a result of an agrarian reform, Manolaki loses even more acreage. The peasants, however, remain dissatisfied, and demand yet another field close to Manolaki's house, so that his "territory" would shrink, as well as his horse-breeding and sheep-farming. He now has to sell livestock in order to pay his debts.

Manolaki is an old, ailing widower who lives on the farm with his son Tosho (from a first marriage) and his daughter Nona, born of a second wife, Antitsa. There is little he can do about the growing conflict with the peasants. In fact, he has no control whatever over the events leading to his final destruction: he is simply an agonized and bewildered landowner. This somber scenario is combined with two additional and important plot lines: Nona and her love affair with Lieutenant Galchev; and social unrest and its possible resolution. All these plot components run in parallel through the whole novel, and only at the end do they interact with one another closely. Of the two children, Tosho remains a colorless and secondary character, while Nona achieves prominence as the novel's heroine. Nona is the only protagonist in the novel who tries to shape her own destiny.

Manolaki's daughter is young and attractive. She is tied to both the past and the present by many subtle, mysterious and almost invisible bonds. Her mother, Antitsa, has long been dead, but her memory still lives on the farm. A poor peasant girl, Antitsa was supposed to marry Gurdyu, one of Manolaki's farmhands; but when Manolaki saw her he was so struck by her beauty that he made her the lady of the house. After becoming Manolaki's lawful wife Antitsa never forgot her social origins. She helped the poor, and showed kindness and generosity to the common people. Now her memory has grown into a legend, but a legend not without its dark spots. Rumor has it that she continued her relationship with Gurdyu after being wed to Manolaki, and apparently there were also two other men in her life. Nona tries to untangle the enigma of her mother's life, and gradually learns that the rumors about the relationship between Antitsa and Gurdyu had some foundation. The unyielding hatred still existing between Manolaki and Gurdyu seems to confirm Nona's findings, and yet she cannot regard her mother as having been a sinner. Among the people Antitsa's name has become the synonym for goodness, and she did whatever she did for the sake of human happiness. "O, mother," whispers Nona to herself, "you are not a sinner, you are a saint."[4]

Nona also discovers that whenever she is on the farm she tries to behave as her mother did. Consciously or unconsciously, she imitates Antitsa to the point of becoming her double. She resembles her mother physically; she tries to be charitable; she even wears her mother's clothes, and she has three men in her life: Jean, Galchev and Yosif. In the course of the novel, Nona's mysterious ties with her mother alternate with her connections to the real world.

As the novel opens, Nona has arrived to visit the farm. After she graduated from high school, Manolaki sent her to Switzerland for the purpose of finishing her education. While in Switzerland, Nona fell in love with Jean and became his fiancée. Now, back on the farm, Nona has developed new relationships with two men: Yosif, a teacher and communist sympathizer whom she had known before; and Galchev, an officer from the neighboring border post. Her involvment with Yosif is rather superficial; she wants to prove that she can be the first girl to attract his attention. However, her acquaintance with Vladimir Galchev grows into deep attachment and love. As the novel draws to a close, it becomes obvious that Nona will have to break her engagement to Jean. Yet the novel has its own relentless logic of events. As Manolaki's economic situation worsens, both he and Tosho, her half-brother, demand that she marry Jean, who is wealthy and could save the farm from bankruptcy.

This internal family tension coincides with acute social conflict: the outbreak of the so-called September uprising of 1923. The uprising was prepared by the Bulgarian Communist Party, which sought to take advantage of political difficulties and economic crises of the postwar period. It managed to gain limited support in both the cities and the villages, but failed miserably to transform the rebellion into a national revolution. Consequently, the September uprising was suppressed with terrible bloodshed, and went down in history as an example of irresponsible partisanship, one of the most tragic events in modern Bulgarian political life.

The internal narrative span of time in the novel covers a short period from early summer to the autumn of 1923. It is no accident that the destruction of the farm and the tragedy of its inhabitants coincides with the outbreak of the September uprising. For the first time in his writing, Yovkov links individual destinies with social and political events. To be sure, the link is very subtle, scarcely discernible: it consists of Lieutenant Galchev, one of the most interesting characters in the novel. Galchev's individual qualities are revealed, not only through the depiction of his burgeoning love for Nona, but also through fragments from his diary and his general attitude toward his work. As a military man he stays aloof from politics, but he also exhibits a strong sense of social responsibility. At one point he heads off a confrontation between peasants from Senovo and Manolaki's people, who have started to plough a field of disputed ownership. The incident demonstrates Galchev's ability to maintain his impartiality, as well as his ability at moving the crowd towards a peaceful compromise. A similar situation occurs during the uprising, when the Senovo peasants have organized an armed squad. They are determined to take the law into their own hands and seize the land by force. Galchev again tries to prevent violence. He manages to stop their march towards Manolaki's farm; but when he tries to negotiate with the peasants, one of them fires a shot and kills him instantly.

Indirectly, that shot also kills Nona. Unable to recover from this tragedy, determined not to yield to Manolaki's and Tosho's pressure to marry Jean, she commits suicide a few hours before her fiancée arrives from Switzerland. Manolaki dies of a stroke shortly afterward, and the farm is sold.

Ironically, by shooting Galchev the rebel peasants killed someone who was sympathetic to their cause and understood their hunger for land. In fact, he had outlined a program of agrarian reform which would have eliminated or at least alleviated class divisions in the Bulgarian village. In the diary that he began to keep shortly before his death, Galchev noted that the peasants could be divided into three groups: the poor, the owners of middle-sized farms, and the rich. The last two strata need no help, but the poor should be allowed to establish large cooperative farms or *zadrugi*, rural communes based on family ties. Such farms would be created out of land owned by schools, the church and the state. Each peasant joining such a farm would also add his own small portion of land. To avoid bureaucracy, cooperatives would be run on the principle of self-government, and be accountable to their members only. If an individual member inherited some wealth, he would have the right to leave the farm without impediment. If, on the other hand, a rich or middle-sized farmer encountered difficulties, he too would have the right to join a co-op farm. Galchev had no time to fill in the details of his plan. In its general outline it followed the theories of rural forms of life worked out by Bulgarian populists. However, by comparison with populist agrarian concepts, Galchev's plan contained some basic adjustments which made it more palatable. While the populists advocated the universal implementation of their program, promoting the idea of *obshtina* (a rural commune based on democratic self-rule) as the exclusive form of agrarian tenure, Galchev made provision for private ownership of land as well.

In any case, Galchev perceived the dangers arising from unequal distribution of wealth and made a theoretical effort to eliminate them. In other words, Galchev sought a peaceful elimination of acute social tensions through the initiation of social reform.

The Farm at the Frontier presents two possible solutions. One is implicit in the plot itself, and implies radical confrontation between opposing social forces. Its spokesman is Yosif, who preaches hatred and destruction of the old order. But the plot of the novel seems also to suggest that this solution is detrimental to the general social good because it allows or even encourages the killing of people such as Galchev, an intelligent and honest man committed to the improvement of society by peaceful means. Violent revolution is unacceptable, at least to Galchev; and I am inclined to believe that Galchev's views on the agrarian question are very similar to Yovkov's own.

In the last two or three decades Bulgarian criticism has stressed the importance of Yovkov as a writer of universal human values,[6] as a moralist who wished to arouse people's consciences and make them respond to human suffering. At the same time, Bulgarian critics have carefully avoided analyzing Yovkov's positive social concepts since they stood clearly in opposition to the Marxist interpretation of history and social conflict as a process of class struggle. Shortly after the Second World War, Ivan Meshekov accused Yovkov of propagating the reactionary idea of social slavery.[7] To condemn Yovkov, though, would mean to deprive Bulgarian literature of a great writer, and so these critics have preferred to ignore the embarrassing aspects of Yovkov's writing.

In fact, though, these aspects cannot and should not be omitted in any discussion of Yovkov's works, because they add to their richness. From the time he first presented himself to the public as a serious writer, Yovkov occasionally exhibited a concern for social questions. One may reject the solutions he suggests, but one cannot deny that he was a keen analyst of social conflicts. They worried him, and he never discussed them without suggesting solutions for them, which was certainly his prerogative. In *The Harvester*, he pictured both the intrusion of new technology into village life (the collective purchase of a threshing machine) and growing social tensions. Yovkov seems to accept — or at least not to oppose — technological progress, but he is obviously disturbed by class divisions. In *The Harvester* he seeks to eliminate them by speaking out in favor of the Christian principle of "loving your neighbor" and the Tolstoyan belief in non-resistance to evil by force. In *The Farm at the Frontier* he presents a solution congruent with the political program of the Radical Party, of which he was a card-carrying member; and in *An Ordinary Person* he resolves class conflicts in urban society in the spirit of utopian socialism. All Yovkov's suggested remedies look to traditional, patriarchal relationships as a model, though they are modified and adjusted to the demands of modern social theories. All three patterns incorporate his basic desire to avoid bloodshed and prevent unnecessary suffering. Should any writer be condemned for that? In fact, the three works just mentioned reflect not only Yovkov's adherence to humanitarian ideals, but also his esthetic credo as visionary realist. Yovkov could not live without dreams and hopes, and therefore embedded them in his literary creation.

II *A WOMAN'S HEART* AND *IF THEY COULD SPEAK*

As Professor Moser has noted, "For all his efforts in the novel and the drama, Yovkov by no means abandoned the short story in the 1930's."[8] He wrote short stories consistently throughout the last seven years of his life, publishing most of them in *Zora*, the official daily of the Radical Party. Later he collected them in two consecutive volumes: *A Woman's Heart* (1935) and *If They Could Speak* (1936).

Apparently Yovkov was a bit dissatisfied with the first title when he discovered that at least two or three other Bulgarian writers had used the word "heart" in book titles at about the same time. One of them was the great poetess Elisaveta Bagryana, who in 1936 issued her third volume of poetry under the title *Surtse choveshko* (The Heart of Man). In one of his conversations with Kazandzhiev, Yovkov joked that the word "heart" had become as banal as the word "soul," which "once upon a time" had been misused[9] (presumably Yovkov was thinking of the Symbolist period, when the word "soul" enjoyed an unprecedented popularity). The title might also have been slightly misleading, since it suggested that the volume was devoted to women in general, whereas in fact only a few stories dealt with women as protagonists. However, if one recalls Yovkov's inclination to treat woman as the incarnation of physical beauty, or more often, as the bearer of positive spiritual values, then the title is justified. The volume covers a range of topics, including compassion, suffering, jealousy, charity, understanding, vengeance and forgiveness. All these emotions are viewed through the prism of what might be called simple human goodness. That is, moralism in the best sense of the word. Moreover, more than any previous volume *A Woman's Heart* demonstrates Yovkov's understanding of life as a dramatic, but not necessarily tragic, phenomenon. Only two of the nineteen short stories in this collection have a clearly tragic tinge: "Vulkadin govori s Boga" (Vulkadin Speaks with God) and "Greshnitsa" (Sinner).

The most powerful story in the volume is "Serafim." The hero, Serafim — a poor wanderer who makes his living by taking occasional light jobs with various employers — reappears in Enyu's coffeehouse after a long absence. At first the owner, on a hot summer's day, sees a stranger approaching in a dirty, worn-out winter coat. After he recognizes him, he greets Serafim as an old acquaintance. The latter tells him of his wanderings and the jobs he has held while gone from the village. Serafim also confesses to Enyu that he managed to save some money for a new winter coat because the old one, as he puts it, "is good only for a museum." Their conversation is interrupted by a woman, who enters the coffeehouse and starts to complain about the high cost of everything. Her husband is ill, and Enyu asks her how he is. She replies that he is not well, and must be examined by a doctor at the hospital. After a while Pavlina (the woman) lowers her voice so that Serafim cannot hear her, but Enyu's loud reply leaves no doubt that she has asked him for money to take her husband to the hospital. Enyu refuses to help her, and Pavlina leaves the coffeehouse in tears.

From a conversation the next day between Enyu and Serafim the reader learns that Serafim has given Pavlina all the money he has saved for the new winter coat. Enyu considers such a deed incomprehensible and rash; he cannot understand how Serafim could offer money to a woman he had just met, and warns him that he may never get his money back. And what of the winter coat he needs so badly? Serafim's reply is terse: "When God gives to her, she will give to me," and he adds that the old coat will last for some time yet.

Thus in Pavlina's life there has appeared an "angel" at a time of need, as his very name implies.

In "Roydyu" the main character is known for his cunningly dishonest ways of fleecing people out of money or possessions. But Roydyu is also unpredictable in his behavior. When people expect him to be mean, he has proven to be good, and vice versa.

Now Roydyu stands accused of stealing money from a peddler who was selling brass pots for water. Roydyu asserts his innocence, but a police search produces undeniable proof: money hidden under a brood hen. Roydyu is compromised, and this event constitutes a turning point in his life. He falls ill and in depression cannot sleep. At the same time Roydyu asks often about his sister-in-law and nephews, and it develops that after the death of Roydyu's older brother he had concealed the fact that some land they had bought together was paid equally by both of them. Instead Roydyu had represented himself as the sole owner of the land, and the sister-in-law as his debtor. Now, after the incident with the peddler, Roydyu fully avows his misdeed: he decides to reveal his swindles and thus cleanse his conscience. As soon as he does so, he falls into a long and healthful sleep. Roydyu has not only abandoned the way of evil, but also helped a poor widow.

The story "Plateno" (Paid) belongs to the same group. Here

a miser named Todor Oprev takes every opportunity to persuade his neighbors that he is as poor as a church mouse. At one point in the past he had borrowed a considerable sum of money from a fellow peasant named Peno, who then died without telling anyone of the debt owed him, so that Todor feels he can get away with refusing Peno's widow when she applies to him for a loan. Then one evening Todor is trapped in his home by an escaped convict, who demands his money or his life, and he is saved only by the providential appearance of two policemen, who frighten the convict away. Afterwards the shaken Todor learns that the police had been sent to his house by Peno's widow after she had a brief vision of her late husband in a dream, although the dream had nothing to do with the situation in which Todor found himself. Moved by his narrow escape, Todor returns to Peno's widow the money which he had been on the point of appropriating for himself.[10]

It should be added that in "Paid" the theme just described is closely interwoven with the motif of supernatural intervention in human affairs, an important motif throughout A Woman's Heart, and especially in such stories as "Stari khora" (Old People) and "Vulkut" (The Wolf).

A distinct niche in this collection is occupied by "Vulkadin Speaks with God," a typical tale of woe in which there intersect both personal misfortune and national trauma which make up the tragedy of the old peasant Vulkadin. His three sons have returned from the war, but with their characters changed beyond recognition. From obedient and loving sons they have become ill-natured, quarrelsome and aggressive individuals. To ease tensions in the family Vulkadin carries out an earlier promise to divide the farm among them. But they must endure yet another and even more painful division, the only negative consequence of the war. The Romanians have returned to seize a part of the land which Vulkadin owned (that is, Dobrudzha). The new border cuts just across his farmland, dividing it into Romanian and Bulgarian parts. His youngest son, Milen, receives the part on the Romanian side of the border, and becomes a "foreigner." This, however, is not the end of Vulkadin's ill fortune. The two eldest sons die, Atanas of a mysterious sickness, and Nikola killed by an assassin's hand. Then Milen is arrested by the Romanians, beaten and released, but later dies from the injuries inflicted on him. Vulkadin loses heart. He refuses to speak to anybody, withdraws into himself, becomes totally indifferent to everything. But he does not stop asking God questions. Who are the people who govern the world? Who gives them power over others? Do they have a God? But his most bitter question is how can a border be drawn so that it separates the graves of ancestors from their living descendants? Why is it that when you visit your brother or son a foreign soldier meets you with a leveled rifle? Vulkadin finds no answers to these questions. When the wife on his youngest son visits him to ask forgiveness and blessing for her remarriage, he does not want to speak to her. He does not object to her marriage, but he will not talk to anyone except God. His alienation is so total as to border on insanity. Vulkadin's life is scarred by war, death and foreign occupation. He embodies the tragedy of a whole generation that endured the calamity of the wars of 1912–1918.

Equally tragic is the lot of Slavenka in "Sinner." The young woman and her husband live in accordance with the traditional patriarchal order; that is, she resides with her in-laws. She is oppressed by the stern, ascetic atmosphere of the house. Ivanitsa, the mother-in-law, spies on Slavenka, and Burni, the husband, beats her because he suspects her of carrying on an affair with another man. And Slavenka, indeed, commits the "sin" of loving a handsome gypsy. She cannot control her feelings and decides to elope with him. But the law — be it "official" or sanctioned by tradition — does not protect Slavenka. She is captured by gendarmes and brought back to face the hatred of the family and her husband's vengeance. She is trapped between the imperatives of her love and the rigid dictates of rules which block its fulfillment. It seems that whenever feminine emotions are at stake, Yovkov parts company with patriarchal ethical rigidity and upholds the rights of the woman. In such instances, he depicts the puritanical cult of chastity as a soulless set of rules which crush genuine human feeling. Those who defend such rules are negatives; but those who transgress them are beautiful and generous.

Finally, we may consider briefly a story which may be termed highly Yovkovian in the sense that it suggests a solution to human unhappiness through spiritual metamorphosis. In "Skitnikut" (The Wanderer), Dafin has spent thirteen years in jail for murdering a man. In committing this crime he was motivated by hatred. Now, released from prison, he is seized by a thirst for vengeance, and decides to return to the village where he had worked for Yorgake as farmhand. Yorgake had not only urged him to kill the man (who was the mayor of the village and his enemy), but he also failed to pay Dafin for the last year of his work. On his way back, Dafin by chance finds himself in a home where the head of the household has died, leaving his wife alone with four children. Dafin offers her his help. Gradually he gets accustomed to his new job, and becomes the breadwinner for the family. The widow is grateful, and asks him to stay with them. It dawns upon Dafin that his mission in life should not be to seek vengeance, but to assure a decent living for helpless people. Once more in Yovkov's prose charity and forgiveness displace the drive for vengeance and destruction.

It has been argued that the last volume of Yovkov's prose published in his lifetime is not a collection of short stories but a novel. The poet Atanas Dalchev once made a remark which supports my previous observation about Yovkov's desire to write a novel, in offering a general assessment of Yovkov as a prose writer:

> Yordan Yovkov did not want to be known as a storyteller only, his lifelong ambition was to write a novel; however, all his efforts in this area ended without success. Despite a dozen impressive descriptive pages, *The Farm at the Frontier* is a failed, sentimental novel with an artificial heroine and unin-

teresting plot. Even less successful is *Gorolomov*. However, shortly before his death Yovkov published *If They Could Speak*; and this collection of short stories, I think, is his genuine novel, the novel about a farmstead which he had vainly tried to create earlier.[11]

The question of whether *If They Could Speak* is a novel is not so important. What is important, however — this is something Bulgarian literary critics have somehow overlooked — is the fact that in this work Yovkov created a masterpiece which it is not easy to define in generic terms. It reflects Yovkov's bias of long standing against strictly defined literary genres as established over the centuries. Should his *Chronicles* be termed *feuilletons*, sketches, or (at least some of them) short stories? Are his war prose pieces merely the literary impressions of a talented reporter, or the well-structured short stories of a creative writer? Yovkov seemed to care little about such questions. Whether by intuition or by reflection he kept pace with the tendency of twentieth-century literature to dispense with clear genre distinctions. On the one hand, Yovkov's prose is the result of a genuine effort to create large epic wholes; on the other, it tends toward constant fragmentation. This tendency reaches a peak in *If They Could Speak*. These short stories exhibit a strong unity of setting, continuity of time and constant recurrence of characters, all of which point toward the novel. Yet at the same time the cycle is divided into shorter structural units which display the indispensable characteristics of the short story genre.

Much the same may be said of the content of this volume. The personal pronoun "they" in the title refers to animals, and this is not a new theme in Yovkov's prose. Earlier I discussed Yovkov's admiration for Lazarov's sculpture "They Overcame," which symbolized the unity between the Bulgarian peasant and his closest helper, the ox. In "Grekhut na Ivan Belin" (The Sin of Ivan Belin), from *Evenings at the Antimovo Inn*, the writer introduces the motif of "if they could speak" for the first time as he describes a she-wolf as a thinking creature with "a look in the eyes which lacks only words."[12] The wolf tries to steal a sheep from Ivan Belin's flock, and in her efforts reminds the writer of a mother who suffers when she cannot provide food for her children. This same motif occurs in "The Doe" from *Balkan Legends*; those who saw the doe at close range would tell others that "its eyes were also like the eyes of a human being."

In *If They Could Speak*, Yovkov focuses on the two motifs mentioned above: a) the interconnected destinies of men and animals on earth, and consequently b) the personification of animals.

The world Yovkov creates in these twenty-three short stories is bounded by the people and animals who live on a farm owned by Zakhari. There are

three farmhands, Mitush, Ago and Marin, the shepherds Petur and David-
ko, the land-steward Vasil, his wife Galunka and her sister Vasilena. Life
on the farm follows its usual course: there are the small quarrels among the
farmhands, the everyday worries of Galunka, the marriage and widowhood
of Vasilena, and her short-lived hope of becoming Zakhari's wife; in short,
there is friendship and occasional enmity as well among people. By and
large, however, the farm is an oasis of serenity. But human affairs form only
a background for the main theme: the presentation of the animal world.

Most often Yovkov describes oxen and horses — the animals closest to
man's toil — then dogs and wild animals (wolves first), and fowl, such as
hens, geese and ducks. He penetrates both the inner relationships between
the animals themselves and the bonds that bind them to human beings. In
most cases the reader is asked to infer an animal's thoughts from its behavior. The medium used to express their "thoughts" and "feelings" most
directly is the oldest farmhand, Mitush, a kind of *alter ego* of the author
himself. In the story "Vseki s imeto si" (Everyone With His Name), Mitush
compares oxen with humans:

> To tell you the truth I hold cattle in higher esteem than man. Is there a better
> creature than the ox, pray tell? You walk by it, it will not bite you, it won't
> kick you. They say it gores ... it doesn't gore! You can drive it as much as you
> want, it will endure, it won't say "oh," it won't say "I can't." It may fall
> down, but it will still keep on.[13]

A little bit later he continues:

> What do you think? But oxen are more clever than you and I. Look, you
> harness them; as soon as you say *kosh!* they put their necks in the collar
> themselves.[14]

In the story "Pri svoite si" (Towards Home), Mitush scolds Ago for beating
an ox, which he says is like beating a child. Like a child, it does not know
what is right, and one must teach it:

> Why beat it? It has a soul too. If cattle could speak, they would be like us.
> Even better than us. What do you know about it? They understand every-
> thing, only they have no language.[15]

In the village where Mitush was born, oxen were called "angels." "They are
like brothers," says Mitush. "They work as we do, and they will die as we
die."[16] When Mitush falls ill and nears death, he goes to the cattle-shed to
bid farewell to his "brother" oxen.

Animals have their individual characteristics, sometimes even eccentric
ones. The dog Zhulturko in "Skitnikut" (Wanderer) displays a certain "ego-
ism": it cares only for itself, it behaves just as it pleases, and it likes to

"travel." Zhulturko vanishes from the farm for longer or shorter periods of time, then reappears and starts the cycle anew. In the story's final episode, a wounded Zhulturko returns home after a long absence and looks at Mitush "with sorrowful and human eyes."

In certain other stories, Yovkov's narrator makes no comments at all, limiting himself to the role of an observer. In "Borba do smurt" (Struggle to the Death) an unusually large wolf does damage to the farm by killing sheep and attacking horses. The shepherd Petur's only hope lies in his dog Anadolets, and the dog indeed understands its task. Both animals are large and vicious, and when they clash there can be no compromise. At one point Petur doubts whether the wolf can be frightened away or killed by Anadolets, and he decides to use a trap. One night, as both animals are fighting, Anadolets is caught in the trap. Before he dies, however, he inflicts mortal wounds on the wolf, and it dies as well.

To render the atmosphere of tension between the two animals and to show the course of their struggle without resorting to direct narrative comment or explanation calls for a great skill on the writer's part. Indeed, the gift of observation, an indispensable condition of realistic expression, is evident in every story in this volume. Especially for those who can remember the charms of village life, this gift may provide ineffable esthetic pleasure. A few examples will illustrate the point. A description of a gander in "Divachka" (Savage) reveals Yovkov's unusual ability to capture the most typical movements and postures of this domestic bird. When the gander sees a stork, the gander "curiously observes with one eye upwards, comes again to stand on one leg, and begins to nap." While Galunka feeds grain to the hens, all the birds form a single group. Sometimes a hen, "pecked by another, jumps and utters a shriek." After a long confinement a mare named Aya is allowed to come out of the stable and "with *raised tail* [italics mine], strained itself and without any difficulty jumped over a high stone wall." Whenever Yovkov describes the appearance, posture, or movements of oxen, his observations are even more striking and precise. There is no need to gather further examples, although we should mention that these scenes all add to the colorful depiction of pastoral life on the farm.

But inexorable modern social developments bring even this corner of quiet patriarchal happiness to its end. In the last story in the collection, "Posledna sreshta" (Last Meeting), Zakharko sells the farm and all its inhabitants depart. "Last Meeting" turned out to have a symbolic meaning for Yovkov himself, because it was also his "last meeting" with readers in his lifetime. The story was published on June 28, 1936. No others appeared after that date.

III *GOROLOMOV'S ADVENTURES*

Yovkov's last novel remained unfinished. Its first four chapters were published in 1931, and the next six in 1937, all in the periodical *Bulgarska misul*
(Bulgarian Thought) edited by Mikhail Arnaudov, a great critic, historian
and literary theoretician. The novel was planned for fourteen chapters, and
Yovkov's posthumous manuscripts contained sketches for two other chapters. Thanks to Mrs. Despina Yovkova's meticulous efforts, these chapters
were partly reconstructed from her husband's notes and printed in *Izkustvo
i kritika* (Art and Criticism) as chapter eleven.[17] They were also included as
a sort of appendix (with no numeration) to the final edition of the novel,
which appeared in book form in 1938. After its publication, *Gorolomov's
Adventures* received favorable evaluations from such critics as Petur Dinekov, Georgi Tsanev, and Arnaudov himself.[18] But by and large, the book
was poorly received. It was evaluated even less favorably with the passing
years. I have already cited Dalchev's remarks on the subject. It is also
noteworthy that Sultanov prefers to write about Yovkov's unwritten,
merely planned work rather than *Gorolomov's Adventures*, which he does
not even mention. Does this mean the novel is an artistic failure?

  Of the critics mentioned above, Arnaudov and Dinekov are most helpful
in answering this question. Arnaudov was the first to examine the novel's
literary genesis and to define its specific genre.[19] Dinekov, on the other
hand, warned against any oversimplified interpretation of *Gorolomov's
Adventures*. Arnaudov's contribution consists of pointing out Yovkov's
dependence on Cervantes, and thus indicating the proper direction for all
further formal studies of the novel. Indeed, there are striking similarities
between *Don Quixote* and *Gorolomov's Adventures*. Since it would be
impossible to list them all here, I shall limit myself to listing a few of the
most typical examples to illustrate my point. A short recapitulation of
Gorolomov's Adventures will provide the proper perspective for such a
discussion.

  Like his great Spanish predecessor, Gorolomov disapproves of existing
sociopolitical conditions and wishes to alter them according to his own
very naive, utopian ideas. This general similarity is the most essential point
of affinity between the Bulgarian hero and his Spanish counterpart, and a
point of departure for any further comparisons between them. Once Gorolomov decides to embark on his mission, his life becomes a string of adventures. As he moves from place to place he meets different people and tries
to instill his own conceptions in them. Then certain additional, external, —
or rather formal — similarities recur throughout the entire novel. Before

departing on his journey, Gorolomov, like Don Quixote, changes his name, from Stancho to Stanislav because, as a Bulgarian proverb puts it, "neither Stancho nor Ivancho will make a great man"; he wants to bear a more impressive name. Yovkov's hero displays the same interest in literature that Don Quixote does. He not only reads books, but also contributes articles on literature to the journal *Far* (Lighthouse). One may also mention the role of inns as a setting for the action. In Cervantes the inn has a slightly different structural function: Don Quixote visits the same inn, which is always a point of departure and arrival during his adventures. In Yovkov's novel, there are several inns, and they usually mark either the beginning or the ending points of Gorolomov's adventurous episodes. Both novels depict inns not only as places of stormy discussion, but also as an arena for fights in which both heroes are severely thrashed. In addition, Gorolomov travels by cart harnessed to two horses, and the cart plays the same role[20] as Rosinante, Don Quixote's horse, does — that is, it ties all events and adventures into a consistent narrative whole. Moreover, Stancho Gorolomov has a companion, just as Don Quixote has his Sancho Panza. A peasant, Ivan Vulchev, accompanies his idealistic master and occasionally warns him against letting his fantasy get the better of him. He is as astute as Sancho Panza, and his reasons for travelling with Gorolomov are as material as those of Don Quixote's squire. The latter hopes to receive an island as reward for his faithful service, and Ivan Vulchev expects from Gorolomov a substantial amount of cash.

The literary origins of *Gorolomov's Adventures* lead us to treat Yovkov's novel as a comic prose epic of satirical novel.[21] Cervantes first created a definite type of satirical prose in which the major compositional role is played by the wanderings of a hero and narrative digressions. Many other writers followed him in developing this technique. Behind the seemingly chaotic structure of Laurence Sterne's masterpiece *The Life and Opinions of Tristram Shandy* (1759), one can discover a consistently applied device of digression. In *Dead Souls* (1842), Nikolay Gogol has Chichikov moving from one locality to another and making absurd transactions involving "dead souls." And Dickens, in his *Posthumous Papers of the Pickwick Club* (1837), sends Mr. Pickwick to various parts of England, and builds the novel as a succession of loosely connected prose pieces.

There is good reason to believe that Yovkov was well acquainted with such masterpieces of world literature as these, with the possible exception of *Tristram Shandy*. He was a great admirer of Gogol's; and where Cervantes is concerned, his best friend, the poet Dimitur Podvurzachov, was the first Bulgarian translator of *Don Quixote*, and we know that Yovkov discussed both the novel and the translation with Podvurzachov on many occasions. Obviously Yovkov used the technique of wanderings and digressions because it allowed him to expose his hero to various situations, so that he should participate in many events and meet a great number of people. Thus the writer enjoyed almost endless opportunities to create many types of humor, which he exploited to the full. Humor of situations abuts on humor of characters; parody appears next to grotesque; irony is entwined with travesty. From beginning to end the stylistic dominant of *Gorolomov's Adventures* remains comic deformation.

One of the most frequent forms of such deformation is the grotesque. In Chapter Three, Gorolomov arrives in a village where peasants are expecting a judge who will resolve a dispute over the ownership of a field (a familiar motif in Yovkov), and they take Gorolomov for that judge. Gorolomov delivers a lofty and florid speech in which he condemns judges and lawyers generally for their greed, and also reprimands the peasants for their inability to solve their own problems. Gorolomov's behavior causes astonishment: nobody understands why he is there. When Gorolomov sees the group of people, he seizes the opportunity to try out his oratorical gifts, to satisfy his passion for making political speeches. The peasants, on the other hand, have gathered to seek justice. This creates a grotesque situation because the participants in it have such different motivations. When the peasants realize that they are being taken in by Gorolomov, they want to beat him, and he must run for his life. This episode also contains elements of parody inherent in the speech itself, which is so vague and so demagogic in content that, when Gorolomov finishes speaking, one peasant asks him to what party he belongs.

There are also numerous examples of irony scattered throughout the novel. One is to be found on the first page, where the writer describes a character as a "harmless socialist." In many instances the irony is directed against Gorolomov, especially when he tries to present himself as a reformer.

Thus far I have discussed the literary affinities and artistic aspects of Yovkov's novel. We should now ask whether *Gorolomov's Adventures* is an unconscious or conscious imitation of *Don Quixote*. Is Gorolomov proof of Yovkov's slavish dependency on the work of another writer? By no means. In creating a modern Don Quixote whose noble intentions are shattered against the wall of human indifference, Yovkov made a *conscious* effort to imitate his great Spanish forerunner. In other words, in this case we are dealing with not a simple instance of influence in the traditional meaning of the word, but an intentionally applied device of literary allusion. Yovkov makes a deliberate reference to Cervantes' novel in order to emphasize his own perception of the contemporary world and the main ideas of his own work. He deliberately creates episodes and situations that leave no doubt as to whom the reader should turn if he wants to understand the philosophical or social implications of the novel.

The first chapter bears an almost symbolic title: "Kum selo" (Towards the Village). It introduces the reader to the book and foreshadows its content: Gorolomov, seized by reformatory zeal and disappointed with his life in the city, decides to spread his message among the peasants and move to the country. To this end, he accepts a job as travelling salesman for the Rila insurance company, and sets out on his journey. Gorolomov believes in the traditional "goodness" of the peasantry, and he is convinced that his speeches possess an unusual power which eventually will bring the peasants to accept his ideas. What ideas does Stancho-Stanislav Gorolomov preach? Like Don Quixote, who wanted to revive the tradition of knight-errantry, Gorolomov has an *idée fixe* of spreading learning among the peasantry. At the same time, however, he is unprepared for his mission because he is himself a "half-educated" man, who possess no more than superficial knowledge. Some have suggested that Yovkov wanted to satirize the kind of intelligentsia which pretends to play a leading role in society but is intellectually incapable of truly doing so. Thus Ivan Meshekov has concluded that Yovkov's novel is yet another critique of modern civilization.[22] Petur Dinekov, however, has warned against such a simplistic interpretation of *Gorolomov's Adventures*, and one should also recall Yovkov's own remark to Kazandzhiev: "In fact, my Gorolomov is a tragic individual; he is constantly misunderstood by people and life."[23]

Who are the people who misunderstand him? Gorolomov's adventures occur in rural areas, in villages, which means that he meets peasants. He assumes they are good, "unspoiled" because they have been protected from the detrimental influences of civilization. But it turns out they are not. Gorolomov's naive assumption is false. The novel contains many examples of peasant cruelty and ignorance. In fact, many of Gorolomov's ideas are generous and beneficial to the peasants, but they do not understand them and so reject them. Hence his tragedy.

In *Gorolomov's Adventures* Yovkov for the first time took a critical look at Bulgarian village life. He does not mock and criticize Gorolomov alone; he also directs withering criticism at the peasant, at the state and its institutions which demoralize him, and at the corruption of political parties. As a matter of fact, the author tries to show that Gorolomov's methods are too honest. He participates in parliamentary elections as a candidate but loses because his opponent Muglov "buys" votes by promising the electorate material gain. The most cruel episode in the novel occurs at the end. Gorolomov suggests that an artificial lake be built near a village because it would allow the peasants to cope with drought. But when Gorolomov faces the assembly of peasants, they nearly stone him to death. In short, the novel confirms Yovkov's fears as expressed in his conversations with Kazandzhiev: "Unless the nation finds in itself sufficient strength for a new upsurge — all will be lost."[24]

Does this mean that Yovkov altered his perception of reality? There seems to be no doubt about it. But this is a different reality from the one Yovkov described in his short stories. In *Gorolomov's Adventures*, Yovkov presents a new and modern reality, of which he disapproves almost totally. This is why he uses satire. Satire expresses the protest of someone who feels the bitterness of defeat. Yovkov had lost his battle with contemporaneity: that world of patriarchal beauty which he had so cherished in his previous works was gone forever. He sets forth no program, no ideals in *Gorolomov's Adventures*. There is just protest. Moreover, one can also find in this novel an echo of the eternal conflict between the individual and society. Gorolomov, among many other things, is a dreamer — a comic dreamer, to be sure — because he is "good," and so he will never find understanding from his contemporaries. He is simply too "strange."

Is, then, *Gorolomov's Adventures* a failure unworthy of much attention? The answer is contained in the preceding discussion. Yovkov did not merely create a new literary hero in Bulgarian literature, as Arnaudov has suggested. He also raised in this novel certain fundamental questions of importance for his country, and even for all mankind. These traits of *Gorolomov's Adventures* prove that, even at the end of his life Yovkov was searching for new artistic solutions and different approaches to life. Such a writer deserves every reader's admiration.

Conclusion

Yovkov's place in the history of Bulgarian literature is in many ways exceptional. Through his work Bulgarian literature in general, and Bulgarian prose in particular, have attained international standards of achievement. The great German writer Thomas Mann included Yovkov's story "The Sin of Ivan Belin" in his anthology *Die schönsten Erzählungen der Welt* (The Most Beautiful Stories of the World, 1956), the only story in Balkan literature so honored. Ivo Andrić, the Yugoslav Nobel Prize winner for literature (1963), has acknowledged his indebtedness to Yovkov, who, he believes, possesses an unusual ability to raise regional values to the level of universal significance.

Scholars from many countries have studied various aspects of Yovkov's prose. There exists in American criticism a penetrating evaluation of Yovkov's place in the history of Bulgarian literature.[1] Charles Moser has defined Yovkov's location in Bulgarian literature using certain "intellectual and literary coordinates," such as Pessimism/Optimism or Nationalism/Internationalism. He assesses Yovkov's contribution to literature through a concrete juxtaposition of his attitude to these questions with that of other Bulgarian writers. The analysis clearly shows Yovkov's innovative treatment of these themes, his opposition to prevailing views on the future, on the historical destiny of his country, on human relationships. Yovkov definitely rejected pessimism in favor of thoughtful optimism. However, the latter is always linked in Yovkov's philosophy with the acceptance and even cultivation of a national cultural tradition which gives individuals the strength to surmount problems in difficult historical times. Without respect for one's own national values, Yovkov argued, there can be no question of survival. A people should strive to develop a sense of national pride, without which a nation can achieve nothing positive. Discovering positive elements to build on should be accompanied by a rejection of thoughtless imitation of other European nations, of the process which has been sometimes defined as "Europeanization." The search for positive values requires penetrating to the very depth of the Bulgarian soul. The writer adhered to this principle in his own literary endeavors, and this is why he was upset by a strong tendency toward national, social and cultural nihilism in Bulgarian letters. Yovkov mounted a bitter attack against Aleko Konstantinov (1863–1897), a Bulgarian prose writer who created a negative image of the Bulgarian in his novel *Bay Ganyo* (1895), by depicting him as an uneducated and totally uncivilized boor. Yovkov once said of *Bay Ganyo*:

It played a dirty role in the evolution of our nation. The Bulgarian does not possess European manners in eating. He does not wash himself as a European does. What of it? Is this the heart of a nation? And should the Bulgarian have such an image of himself in his own consciousness? This paralyzes him. The Bulgarian began to think that he should imitate Europeans, to become European; and he began to be ashamed of his own way of life, to laugh at it. Consequently, he severed his ties with everything national, with the traditional, and there occurred a shift in the Bulgarian's soul which we regret and seek to correct.[2]

As a creative writer Yovkov devoted his whole life to the search for the unique specificity of his nation's spirit. In so doing he turned to the deepest and most authentic layers of Bulgarian society, that is, to the peasantry, with its folkloristic, patriarchal tradition and culture. However, it should be stressed that the Yovkovian cult of tradition was not translated into artistic traditionalism on either the thematic or formal levels of his creative effort. Paradoxically, in his desire to define the specific characteristics of the nation he loved so much, Yovkov also defined the human and universal dimensions which link Bulgarians with the rest of mankind. Love and goodness, sorrow and joy, dream and reality are closely interwoven in the whole of Yovkov's prose. The peasant from "Along the Wire" will forever symbolize man's hope of happiness, and Yovkov will always be the writer of hope. Yovkov's greatest contribution to Bulgarian literature, his indisputable strength as a writer, lies in his creation of a new character as bearer of certain moral and philosophical values. Never before had a Bulgarian writer created a protagonist who was unconcerned with social, patriotic or political issues of the day. His localized heroes are preoccupied with universal human problems. They suffer, and they are ready to die for love; they are prepared to sacrifice for others, to evince charity; they long for beauty. Many of Yovkov's characters experience exhausting internal struggles before reaching decisions, but as a rule their decisions lead to their personal improvement. This innovative treatment of characters within the framework of Bulgarian literature constitutes Yovkov's most obvious link with universal values of world literature. In creating his "small" characters from remote Dobrudzha, Yovkov opened the door for Bulgarian literature to join the great family of world literature.

Yovkov's significance as a writer continues to grow. Time and evolving reality have continually confirmed the wisdom of his poetical vision. Although he based his writing on a cult of the past, Yovkov at the same time was in many respects very modern. His treatment of relationships between men and women leaves no doubt that he perceived the changes facing contemporary society, and also leaves no doubt where his sympathies lay. In Yovkov's perception of the world, woman is equal to man, an independent being with the right to pursue her own happiness, to search for love, to choose freely her partner in life. However, Yovkov ignored the sexual aspect of human relationships. Although physical attractiveness plays an important role in his concept of beauty, man-woman relationships are based on idealistic foundations. Yovkov may be considered a forerunner of the contemporary process of emancipation for women.

Finally, what impact did Yovkov have on the later development of Bulgarian literature? Despite political and social developments in Bulgaria unfavorable to him, Yovkov's prose caught the imagination of many writers who came after him. Angel Karaliychev — though a member of the prewar generation — reminds us of Yovkov with his tendency to depict characters in their close association with nature, and with his obvious preference for simple and poor people. Others — such as Ivaylo Petrov, Iliya Volen and Yordan Radichkov — who became known or started their literary careers after World War II, tried to develop some of Yovkov's philosophical and esthetic beliefs. Petrov and Volen often describe the uncanny wisdom of Bulgarian peasants in a Yovkovian manner, while Radichkov presents their innate optimism and genuine inventiveness. All these writers have benefited from the linguistic and stylistic richness of Yovkov's prose, and have recognized its close connection with folklore. These writers — who are today among the most significant authors in Bulgarian literature — have grasped the most essential aspect of Yovkov's artistic experience: its roots in Bulgarian folklore. Thus Yovkov effected a true artistic upheaval in Bulgarian literature — he taught others to use the national cultural treasure that is the inborn, spontaneous creative achievement of the peasantry.

As for Yovkov's philosophical and ethical ideas, not all of them have withstood the pressure of time. This does not necessarily mean that they have become entirely obsolete. Yovkov's belief in human nobility and goodness, his faith in man's capacity for spiritual self-improvement, will remain an everlasting monument to his moral integrity.

NOTES

Chapter 1

1. This misinformation about Yovkov's date of birth appeared for the first time in 1919 in the literary anthology *Zhutva* (Harvest), where the date of Yovkov's birth is given as November 8, 1884 (p. 38).

2. As early as 1932, Vasil Todorov, a teacher from Yovkov's native village of Zheravna, wrote an article "Istinata okolo datata na razhdaneto na nashiya pisatel Yordan Yovkov" (The Truth About the Birthdate of Our Writer Yordan Yovkov), and sent it to the well-known scholar Mikhail Arnaudov. But Yovkov raised objections, and the article never appeared in print. For more on this see Spiridon Kazandzhiev, *Sreshti i razgovori s Yordan Yovkov* (Meetings and Conversations with Yordan Yovkov) (Sofia, 1960), p. 69.

3. As soon as Yovkov learned about Todorov's article, he wrote him a letter asking him to abandon the idea of publishing it. He admitted, though, that "everything [that Todorov wrote] was true." Yovkov's letter to Todorov was reprinted in Dimo Minev's documentary collection *Yordan Yovkov. Spomeni i dokumenti* (Yordan Yovkov. Recollections and Documents) (Varna, 1969), pp. 21–22.

4. Georgi Konstantinov, *Tvortsi na Bulgarskata literatura* (Writers of Bulgarian Literature) (Sofia, 1941), p. 200.

5. This is the title of the first edition, published in Varna in 1947. The second, enlarged edition appeared in 1969, under the title given in footnote three.

6. Danail Konstantinov, *Zheravna v minaloto i do dneshno vreme* (Zheravna in the Past and Present) (Zheravna, 1948), p. 511. The reference to the etymology of the name is on pp. 60–61.

7. The historical past of Zheravna can be traced as far back as Thracian times. Later it fell under Roman domination. The territory of present day Bulgaria was invaded by Slavs, Tartars, and Goths. The latter left the territory, and the first Bulgarian Empire was formed of Slavs and Tartars. It lasted until approximately the tenth century, when it was conquered by the Greeks, and Zheravna fell under Byzantine or — as the Bulgarians call it — Greek domination.

8. Wherever possible the English titles are taken from Professor Charles Moser's *A History of Bulgarian Literature* (The Hague and Paris, 1972), and his article "The Visionary Realism of Jordan Yovkov," *The Slavic and East European Journal* XI (1967), no. 1.

9. See Minev, p. 26.

10. *Poturi* are full-buttoned, broad, tight-legged breeches made of thick woolen material.

11. *Saltamarka* — a kind of sleeveless jacket, a doublet.

12. Dobrudzha is a historical and geographic region in the lower Danube River plains. It is bordered on the east by the Black Sea; the Danube River constitutes the northern and northwestern frontier of the region, while the Batova River valley limits it from the south. The southwestern boundary remains unclear. As soon as

Romania and Bulgaria regained their independence in the nineteenth century, Dobrudzha became a bone of contention between them. According to an agreement reached by the Romanian and Bulgarian governments in 1940, Dobrudzha was divided into Northern Dobrudzha, which remained in Romania, and Southern Dobrudzha, which was returned to Bulgaria but from 1919 to 1940, the whole of Dobrudzha belonged to Romania.

13. The Bulgarian school system at that time was composed of three stages: four years of elementary school, three years of junior high school, or *gymnasium*. In other words, the students took the examination for the secondary school certificate in the eleventh grade.

14. According to D. Konstantinov, after leaving Zheravna Yovkov visited the place twice, but only to spend his vacations between 1898 and 1900. See D. Minev, p. 48.

15. Information provided by Mrs. Despina Yovkova, Yovkov's wife.

16. See the memoirs by Georgi Vulchev and also Frosa Ivanova, who became acquainted with Yovkov in 1908, both in Minev, p. 113 and p. 120 respectively.

17. The Radical Democratic Party was founded in 1905 as a splinter group from the Democratic Party. It participated in the coalition governments from June 1918 to August 1919. It changed its name to Radical Party in 1922, and ceased to exist in 1949.

18. See Kalina Ivanova-Momova in Minev, *op. cit.*

19. For quite some time the poem "Sudba" (Destiny, 1905), was thought to be Yovkov's first publication. Recently D. K. Boshnakov, in a piece published in *Narodna Kultura* (National Culture) for Nov. 14, 1980, has established the earlier date.

20. See Minev, p. 130.

21. For a detailed discussion of Modernism see Moser's *History of Bulgarian Literature*, Chapter IV "The Age of Modernism and Individualism (1896–1917)", pp. 91–119.

22. Symbolism (sometimes referred to as Neo-Romanticism) in Bulgarian literature was the second stage in the evolution of Modernism. Its first manifestations can be traced back to the very beginning of this century. Peyo Yavorov (1877–1914) is considered to be one of the greatest representatives of Bulgarian Symbolism.

23. Minev, pp. 138–140.

24. They are enumerated in Chapter Two.

25. Simeon Sultanov, *Yovkov i negoviyat svyat* (Yovkov and His World) (Sofia: Bulgarski pisatel), 1968, pp. 184–193.

26. Minev, p. 159.

27. From the diary of Nikola Atanasov, a literary critic (entry of May 8, 1932), published in Minev, p. 227.

28. See Minev, p. 190.

29. In a letter of October 9, 1921, Yovkov wrote: "I lived in a hole (*dupka*), 3 km. from the Legation": Minev, p. 181. See also his letter of September 21, 1927, to the Bulgarian ambassador: *Ibid.*, p. 204.

30. Petur Dinekov, "Poslednite dni na Yordan Yovkov" (The Last Days of Yordan Yovkov), *Plamuk* (Flame), No. 11, 1980, pp. 67–76. Also: V. Ivanov, "Smurtta na Yordan Yovkov" (The Death of Yordan Yovkov), in Minev, pp. 244–246.

Chapter 2

1. "The declaration of war was met with great enthusiasm by the Bulgarian masses," write Bulgarian historians Simitur Kosev, Khristo Khristov, and Dimitur Angelov in their *Kratka istoriya na Bulgariya* (A Short History of Bulgaria) (Sofia, 1962), p. 216.

2. I have tried to establish these points of affinity in my book *Sztuka pisarska Jordana Jowkowa* (The Literary Craft of Yordan Yovkov) (Wroclaw-Warsaw-Cracow, 1964), pp. 31–32.

3. As a matter of fact, this happened immediately after the communist seizure of power in Bulgaria in 1945. Yovkov was condemned not only for his cult of patriarchal and traditional mores, but also for his allegedly "reactionary" defense of official policy in his war prose. This critical evaluation was gradually rectified in the late 1950's, and finally rejected.

4. Sultanov, p. 33.

5. Grigor Vasilev, *Yordan Yovkov. Spomeni i pisma* (Yordan Yovkov. Recollections and Letters) (Sofia, 1940), p. 64.

6. Efrem Karanfilov, "Geroite vuv voennite razkazi na Yordan Yovkov" (The Heroes in the War-Stories of Yordan Yovkov), in his book *Poeziya v prozata* (Poetry in Prose) (Sofia, 1957), pp. 64–65.

7. In his letter to Margaret Harkness of April 1888, Engels makes the following remark about Balzac: "Well, Balzac was politically a Legitimist [that is, an adherent of the Bourbons overthrown in France in 1792 who represented the interests of the feudal aristocracy — E.M.]; his great work is a constant elegy on the irretrievable decay of good society, his sympathies are all with the class doomed to extinction. But for all that his satire is never keener, his irony never bitterer, than when he sets in motion the very men and women with whom he sympathizes most deeply — the nobles." See *Marx and Engels On Literature and Art* (Moscow: Progress Publishers, 1976), pp. 91–92).

8. Leo Tolstoy exercised a great influence on both Bulgarian literature and social thought.

9. Elin Pelin (1877–1949), one of the greatest Bulgarian Realists of a modern persuasion, described the decline of the traditional, patriarchal order and the detrimental effect of greed on human relationships in such short novels as *The Gerak Family* (1911) and *Zemya* (Land: 1922).

10. See Petur Pondev, "Tvorchestvoto na Yovkov" (Yovkov's Writing), an introduction to Yovkov's *Subrani suchineniya* (Collected Works), 7 vols. (Sofia, 1956), I, 17. Further references will be to this edition.

11. Yovkov, I, 428.

12. Solveig is the heroine of Henrik Ibsen's play *Peer Gynt*. After many years Peer Gynt returns to his native village to die at the side of Solveig, whom he had loved as a young man. Throughout all these years she has remained faithful to him.

13. Yovkov, I, 455.

14. *Ibid.*, I, 454.

15. *Ibid.*, I, 459.

16. *Ibid.*, I, 440.

17. *Ibid.*, I, 497.

18. Some remarks on this question may be found in my *Sztuka pisarska Jordana Jowkowa* (The Literary Craft of Yordan Yovkov), pp. 30–40.

19. M. E. Kronegger, *Literary Impressionism* (New Haven, n.d.), p. 154.

20. *Ibid.*, p. 37.

21. Vladimir Vasilev, "Marshut na pobedata i na smurtta" (The March of Victory and Death), in *Zlatorog* (Horn of Plenty), I, 1 (1920), pp. 46–61; and B. J. (probably Boris Jotsov) in a short note published also in *Zlatorog*, IV, No. 1 (1925), p. 54.

22. M. E. Kronegger, *op. cit.*, pp. 38–40.

23. Yovkov, I, 459.

24. Khristo Yasenov (1889–1925), Bulgarian poet who began as a Symbolist and ended as a revolutionary promoting the ideas of the Russian revolution.

25. Yovkov, I, 396.

26. *Ibid.*, I, 489.

27. *Ibid.*, I, 128.

28. *Ibid.*, I, 189.

29. *Ibid.*, I, 529.

30. Mikhail Kremen (1884–1964), Bulgarian prose writer and memoirist. His most important work is *Bregalnitsa* (1920), in which he described his experiences during the Balkan wars.

31. Vladimir Musakov (1877–1916), Bulgarian writer and journalist who gave a moving account of his war experiences in a volume of prose entitled *Kurvavi petna* (Bloody Stains, 1921).

32. Yovkov, I, 359.

33. *Ibid.*, I, 340.

34. Yovkov, II, 190–91.

35. *Ibid.*, II, 259.

Chapter 3

1. Charles Moser, "The Visionary Realism of Jordan Jovkov," *The Slavic and East European Journal*, XI, No. 1 (1967), 44–58.

2. See also Simeon Sultanov, *Yovkov i negoviyat svyat* (Yovkov and His World) (Sofia, 1968), p. 286. On p. 41 the author writes: "In fact, like any great artist he is both Realist and Romantic. As far as external representation is concerned, he is an impeccable Realist; however, if judged by his internal concepts, he is Romantic."

3. Donald Fanger, *Dostoevsky and Romantic Realism: A Study of Dostoevsky in Relation to Balzac, Dickens and Gogol* (Cambridge: Harvard University Press, 1965), p. 307. See especially Chapter One, "Realism, Pure and Romantic."

4. The phenomenon of the intelligentsia is a Slavic one, though also known in the German tradition. The term denotes the educated strata of society, and includes people who make their living in the intellectual professions (lawyers, medical doctors, teachers, and so on).

5. It is interesting to note, though, that the first version of this story was written in the *imperfectum* and *perfectum* of the so-called "recounting tense." An old villager, Vulo, tells the story to the teacher who is passing it on, as it were, to the

reader. The folkloristic viewpoint of the old villager is suppressed by the mediation of the teacher. Yovkov altered this in the second version of the story, reprinted in 1927. He explained the role of the old villager and also recounted the story in the "direct" past imperfect tense. In the first version the narrator is the teacher, but in the second version we clearly have a folkloristic narrator who presents the events from the viewpoint of an old peasant.

6. Moser, "Visionary Realism," p. 49.

7. Spiridon Kazandzhiev, *Sreshti i razgovori s Yordan Yovkov* (Meetings and Conversations with Yordan Yovkov) (Sofia, 1960), p. 34 (entry of September 18, 1930).

8. *Ibid.*, p. 12 (entry of April 21, 1929).

9. *Ibid.*, p. 38 (entry of October 1, 1930), as translated by Moser in "Visionary Realism," p. 47.

10. *Ibid.*, pp. 37–38, as translated by Moser, p. 47.

11. *Ibid.*, p. 38 (translation mine).

12. A detailed account of this story can be found in Moser, "Visionary Realism," pp. 56–57, and also in his *History of Bulgarian Literature* (The Hague: Mouton, 1972), p. 199.

13. Stefan Vasilev, *Esteticheski problemi v tvorchestvoto na Yordan Yovkov* (Esthetic Problems in the Works of Yordan Yovkov) (Sofia: Izdatelstvo na Bulgarska Akademiya na Naukite [Bulgarian Academy of Sciences], 1961), p. 163.

14. See Pantaley Zarev, "Yordan Yovkov," in *Istoriya na bulgarskata literatura* (History of Bulgarian Literature) (Sofia, 1976), IV, 264.

15. Although some of Tolstoy's social theories, I think, are reflected in Yovkov, the whole question needs a thorough examination. The same is true for the problem of Tolstoy's influence on Yovkov in general.

16. Simeon Khadzhikosev, "Pavle Fertigut" i "Serafim" ("Pavle Fertigut" and "Serafim") in *Plamuk* (Flame), XXIV, No. 11 (1980), 151.

17. In the first edition this dream is described in Chapter Fourteen; in the second edition (1930) in Chapter Seventeen. I have based my account of the novel on the first edition (1920). The second one has four additional chapters, but its basic idea remains unchanged.

18. Moser, *A History of Bulgarian Literature*, p. 198.

19. Yovkov, II, 179.

20. The prototype of such a woman appears for the first time in the short story "Fortuitous Guests": "the bride" brings to a military outpost a spirit of gentleness and goodness.

21. Yovkov, II, 173.

22. Minev, pp. 272–273.

23. From a letter to D. Konstantinov, in Minev, p. 276. Yovkov wrote letters to several other people as well in connection with *Balkan Legends*.

24. See my *Sztuka pisarska Jordana Jowkowa*, pp. 54–62.

25. *Kurdzhaliystvo* was a movement which originated within the oppressed Turkish population, but later took in non-Turkish elements as well. The *Kurdzhalii* were robbers who took justice into their own hands: they attacked the rich, whether Bulgarians or Turks, churches and so on. This was the earliest and most spontaneous opposition to the Turkish empire. The activity of the *khayduti* was determined

mainly by national consciousness. It was directed against the Turks and in defense of Bulgarian interests. It would be a mistake, however, to think that the *khayduti* included no criminal elements. Some of them lived by looting the peaceful population. In the second half of the nineteenth century this movement became a more organized force within the Bulgarian national revival. There exists an entire subgenre of folksongs called *khaydushki pesni* (*khayduti* songs).

26. There is one exception: in "Yunashki glavi" (Heroes' Heads) — not a love story but a historical account of a freedom fighter's drama — the father sees his son's head impaled on a stake.

27. Y. Kholevich, "Na kolene pred naroda" (On Your Knees Before the People), *Septemvri* (September), No. 11 (1980), p. 41.

28. Vladimir Vasilev, "Yovkovite trevogi okolo *Staroplaninski legendi*" (Yovkov's Worries over *Balkan Legends*) in *Zlatorog* (Horn of Plenty), No. 9 (1937), pp. 343–351.

29. Elka Konstantinova, "Otnovo v sveta na Yovkov" (Again in Yovkov's World), *Plamuk* (Flame), No. 11 (1980), p. 174.

30. Cz. Zgorzelski, "Über die Strukturtendenzen der Ballade" (On the Structural Tendencies of the Ballad), in: *Zagadnienia rodzajow literackich* (Problems of Literary Genres), II, No. 4, pp. 105–135.

31. Yovkov began to write this collection in 1922, and finished it in 1928. Ten stories were written in the course of a few months in 1927–28, though, as Sultanov puts it (p. 96), "This fast 'birth' was preceded by a long 'pregnancy'."

32. Sultanov, p. 101.

33. Yovkov, III, 286.

34. See Kazandzhiev, pp. 11–12.

35. See Moser, "Visionary Realism," p. 55.

Chapter 4

1. Sultanov, pp. 109–147: "Nepriyatnosti."

2. Kazandzhiev, p. 86 (entry of November 1, 1936); see also p. 71 (entry of September 26, 1932).

3. See Yovkov, VII, 133–34.

4. Sultanov, pp. 114–119.

5. See Yovkov's note published in *Bulgarska rech* (Bulgarian Language), V, No. 2 (November 1930), p. 39. Albena is not involved in killing her husband, and she does not wish any involvement. Yovkov also recalls that he took this motif from real life. When he worked as a teacher in Musubey, Yovkov was present when a woman accused of murder was arrested. He was struck by the fact that in spite of the accusation, she did not lose the sympathy of the villagers. There was also a mill at which, in Yovkov's words, "various events took place."

6. *Literaturen glas* (Literary Voice), No. 161 (September 24, 1932).

7. *Zora* (Dawn), XIV, No. 3971 (September 30, 1932).

8. *Ibid.*

9. Minev, p. 333.

10. Yovkov, VII, 291.

11.   See K. Bliznakova, "Nravstvenite alternativi v piesite na Yovkov" (The Ethical Alternatives in Yovkov's Plays), *Septemvri* (September), No. 11 (1980), p. 57.

12.   Kazandzhiev, p. 36 (entry of September 20, 1930).

13.   For example, Pantaley Zarev, in his survey of Yovkov's writing in *Istoriya na bulgarskata literatura* (History of Bulgarian Literature) (Sofia, 1976), IV, 213–271, merely mentions the title of *The Millionaire*.

14.   For instance, some have wondered whether *Albena* was a drama or not. Vladimir Vasilev, a critic and the editor of *Zlatorog*, refused to call it a drama, which led to a considerable strain in his relationship with Yovkov. See Georgi Konstantinov, *A. Strashimirov, Elin Pelin, Yordan Yovkov — v spomenite na suvremennitsite si* (A. Strashimirov, Elin Pelin, Yordan Yovkov in Reminiscences of Their Contemporaries) (Sofia, 1962), p. 459.

15.   In *Sto godini bulgarski teatur* (One Hundred Years of Bulgarian Theater) (Sofia, 1956), p. 221.

16.   Moser, *A History of Bulgarian Literature* p. 197.

17.   Kazandzhiev, p. 32 (entry of September 12, 1930).

Chapter 5

1.   Kazandzhiev, p. 68 (entry of February 6, 1932).

2.   Sultanov, p. 227.

3.   There exists some doubt as to the historical setting of *Boryana*. By and large critics agree that its dramatic action mixes two temporal planes: that of the prewar and the postwar Bulgarian village.

4.   Yovkov, V, 232.

5.   Bulgarian *narodnitsi* such as Khristo Maximov, Nikofor Popfilipov, and Todor Vlaykov were under the strong influence of the Russian populists. They advocated for the Bulgarian village a sort of democratic, collective self-rule through the *obshtina* (commune), the introduction of machinery in agriculture, and extensive education of the peasantry. Some of these ideas were later incorporated, in modified form, in the program of the Radical Party, of which Yovkov was a member. A few other leading Bulgarian writers — Anton Strashimirov and Todor Vlaykov, for example — were members of this party too. The latter published in 1897 a novel entitled *Kmetove* (Mayors), in which the central character, a teacher, propagated the idea of *obshtina*. For many years Vlaykov edited *Demokraticheski pregled* (Democratic Review), the official literary, cultural and political organ of the Radical Party. The party was sometimes called "the party of educators." Galchev's ideological attitude seems to be an amalgam of the traditional, patriarchal form of rural life known among the South Slavs, with the ideas of the populists and the program of the Radical Party.

6.   Stefan Vasilev, *Esteticheski problemi v tvorchestvoto na Yordan Yovkov* (Esthetic Questions in the Work of Yordan Yovkov) (Sofia: Bulgarska Akademija na naukite, 1961), p. 275.

7.   Ivan Meshekov, *Yordan Yovkov — romantik-realist* (Yordan Yovkov, Romantic and Realist) (Sofia: Golovanov, 1947), p. 276.

8.   Moser, *A History of Bulgarian Literature*, p. 195.

9.   Kazandzhiev, p. 83 (entry of April 13, 1936).

10.   Retelling of the story by Charles Moser in "The Visionary Realism of Jordan Jovkov," *The Slavic and East European Journal*, XI, No. 1 (Spring 1967), p. 54.

11.   Atanas Dalchev, *Fragmenti* (Fragments) (Sofia: Bulgarski pisatel, 1967), p. 7.

12.   Yovkov, III, 341.

13.   *Ibid.*, IV, 230.

14.   *Ibid.*

15.   *Ibid.*, IV, 367.

16.   *Ibid.*, IV, 368.

17.   *Izkustvo i kritika* (Art and Criticism), No. 3 (1938), pp. 239–246.

18.   See the references in my *Sztuka pisarska Jordana Jowkowa,* pp. 92–93.

19.   Mikhail Arnaudov, "Gorolomov. Edin originalen tip u Yovkov" (Gorolomov. An Original Type in Yovkov), in *Y. Yovkov 1814–1937* (Sofia, 1937), pp. 25–29; the second article, "Gorolomov. Edin komichen roman ot Y. Yovkov" (Gorolomov. A Comic Novel by Y. Yovkov), appeared in *Yovkov 1884–1937. Literaturen sbornik* (Y. Yovkov 1884–1937. Literary Collection). Note the incorrect date of Yovkov's birth in both collections.

20.   Knud Togeby, *La Composition du roman "Don Quichotte"* (The Composition of *Don Quixote*) (Copenhagen, 1957), p. 63.

21.   Edward Możejko, "Priklyucheniyata na Gorolomov kato satirichen roman" (*Gorolomov's Adventures* As a Satirical Novel), *Literaturna misul* (Literary Thought), Vol. V, No. 4 (September 1961), pp. 43–60.

22.   Ivan Meshekov, *op. cit.*, p. 156.

23.   Kazandzhiev, p. 96 (entry of June 25, 1937).

24.   *Ibid.*, p. 49 (entry of January 16, 1931).

Conclusion

1.   Charles Moser, "Jovkov's Place in Modern Bulgarian Literature," in *Bulgaria Past and Present. Studies in History, Literature, Economics, Music, Sociology, Folklore and Linguistics* (Columbus, Ohio: American Association for the Advancement of Slavic Studies, 1976), pp. 267–272.

2.   Kazandzhiev, p. 94 (entry of May 20, 1937).

SELECTED BIBLIOGRAPHY

Works

Yordan Yovkov. *Subrani suchineniya* [Collected Works]. ed. Angel Karaliychev, Andrey Gulyashki, Elka Yovkova, Iliya Volen, Simeon Sultanov, with a foreword by Petur Pondev. 7 volumes. Sofia: Bulgarski pisatel [Bulgarian Writer], 1956. The edition used for this book except for the drama *An Ordinary Person*, which is omitted. Contains extensive critical commentaries, identification of some persons, writers and literary characters.
_____. *Razkazi* [Short Stories]. Ed. Tikhomir Tikhov. Sofia: Bulgarski pisatel [Bulgarian Writer], 1962. With an introduction by Petur Dinekov.
_____. *Razkazi v dva toma.* [Short Stories in Two Volumes]. Ed. Iliya Volen. Sofia: Bulgarski pisatel [Bulgarian Writer], 1968.
_____. *Obiknoven chovek* [An Ordinary Person]. Sofia: 1936.

Translations into English

Colombo, John and Nikola Roussanoff. *The Balkan Range: A Bulgarian Reader.* Toronto: Hounslow Press, 1976. Contains "Shibil," "The White Swallow," and "One Bulgarian Woman."
In the Fields: Bulgarian Short Stories. Sofia: Narodna kultura [People's Culture], 1957. Contains "The Stranger" ["Drugoselets"].
Kirilov, Nikolay, and Frank Kirk. *Introduction to Modern Bulgarian Literature.* New York: Twayne, 1969. Contains "Shibil," "The White Swallow," and "Heroes' Heads."

Biographical Materials

Kazandzhiev, Spiridon. *Sreshti i razgovori s Yordan Yovkov* [Meetings and Conversations with Yordan Yovkov]. Sofia: Nauka i izkustvo [Science and Art], 1960. A very interesting and useful account of Kazandzhiev's conversations with Yovkov.
Minev, Dimo. *Yordan Yovkov. Spomeni i dokumenti* [Yordan Yovkov. Recollections and Documents]. Varna, 1969. The second and expanded edition of a book first published in 1947, under a slightly different title. An excellent source of information on Yovkov's biography.
Minkov, Tsvetan. *Yordan Yovkov. Tvorchestvo i zhivot* [Yordan Yovkov. Art and Life]. Sofia, 1939.
Vasilev, Grigor. *Yordan Yovkov. Spomeni i pisma* [Yordan Yovkov. Recollections and Letters]. Sofia, 1940.

Secondary Literature on Yovkov

Arnaudov, Mikhail. "Razkazite na Yordan Yovkov" [The Short Stories of Yordan Yovkov]. *Otechestvo* [Fatherland], III (1916), Nos. 36–37. The first serious discussion of Yovkov's war prose, with an assessment of his work as a writer.

Dinekov, Petur. "Kult kum krasotata u Yovkov" [The Cult of Beauty in Yovkov], *Zlatorog* [Horn of Plenty], XVIII (1937), No. 9. The author, a distinguished literary historian and critic, was the first to point out one of the most important traits of Yovkov's prose: his cult of physical and spiritual beauty.

Meshekov, Ivan. *Yordan Yovkov. Romantik-realist* [Yordan Yovkov. Romantic and Realist]. Sofia, 1947. The author approaches Yovkov as a dogmatic Marxist, accusing him of being a "conservative" or even "reactionary" writer who wants to restore the past.

Moser, Charles. "The Visionary Realism of Jordan Jovkov," *The Slavic and East European Journal*, XI (1967), No. 1. One of the best studies of Yovkov to date. Includes some important biographical data, and analyzes the role of dreams in Yovkov's prose in order to define its most essential feature as "visionary realism."

_____. "Jovkov's Place in Modern Bulgarian Literature," in *Bulgaria Past and Present*, ed. Thomas Butler. Columbus, Ohio: American Association for the Advancement of Slavic Studies, 1976. An assessment of Yovkov's place in the history of Bulgarian literature.

Możejko, Edward. *Sztuka pisarska Jordana Jowkowa* [The Literary Craft of Yordan Yovkov]. Wroclaw-Warsaw-Cracow: Ossolineum, 1964. An analysis of certain aspects of Yovkov's artistic evolution.

Nikolov, Malcho. *Tvorcheskiyat put na Yordan Yovkov* [The Artistic Evolution of Yordan Yovkov]. Sofia, 1938. One of the first systematic discussions of Yovkov as a writer.

Sarandev, Ivan. *V sveta na "Staroplaninski legendi"* [In the World of *Balkan Legends*]. Sofia: Nauka i izkustvo [Science and Art], 1980. A detailed analysis of Yovkov's most important collection of stories.

Sultanov, Simeon. *Yovkov i negoviyat svyat* [Yovkov and His World]. Sofia: Bulgarski pisatel [Bulgarian Writer], 1968. A sensitive work of literary criticism. The author shows a subtle understanding of Yovkov's prose, but unfortunately neglects some of its important aspects.

Vasilev, Stefan. *Esteticheski problemi v tvorchestvoto na Yordan Yovkov* [Esthetic Questions in the Writings of Yordan Yovkov]. Sofia: Bulgarska Akademiya na naukite [Bulgarian Academy of Sciences], 1961. A discussion of Yovkov's writing from the viewpoint of such esthetic categories as the tragic, the beautiful, and so on. At times the author's Marxist philosophy prevents him from taking an objective view of Yovkov.

Vasilev, Vladimir. "Marshut na pobedata i na smurtta" [The March of Victory and Death], *Zlatorog* [Horn of Plenty], Vol. I (1920), No. 1. This leading critic — also the editor of *Zlatorog* — was one of the first to recognize Yovkov's great talent.